2

BUSINESS FLUCTUATIONS AND THE AMERICAN LABOR MOVEMENT 1915-1922

STUDIES IN HISTORY, ECONOMICS AND PUBLIC LAW

EDITED BY THE FACULTY OF POLITICAL SCIENCE
OF COLUMBIA UNIVERSITY

Volume CX] [Number 2

Whole Number 247

BUSINESS FLUCTUATIONS AND THE AMERICAN LABOR MOVEMENT

1915–1922

BY

V. W. LANFEAR

AMS PRESS
NEW YORK

COLUMBIA UNIVERSITY
STUDIES IN THE
SOCIAL SCIENCES

247

The Series was formerly known as
Studies in History, Economics and Public Law

Reprinted with the permission of Columbia University Press
From the edition of 1924, New York
First AMS EDITION published 1968
Manufactured in the United States of America

Library of Congress Catalogue Card Number: 68-57572

AMS PRESS, INC.
NEW YORK, N.Y. 10003

PREFACE

Through making in 1919 a study of the wage awards of the United States labor adjustment boards, the author became interested in the more general question of business conditions and the labor movement, and therefore, at the suggestion of Professor W. F. Ogburn, chose this as the subject for his doctoral dissertation. This choice, however, was made with full recognition of the limitations of any such study. Fragmentary and incomplete data have made it particularly difficult to draw any specific conclusions or to give an unqualified answer to any of the questions that naturally suggest themselves in connection with the business cycle and its social consequences. It is hoped, however, that the tentative results here obtained may be of some slight use as suggesting one method of approach to the consideration of this most vital economic problem.

The author wishes to take this opportunity of thanking Professor W. A. Berridge of Brown University and Alvin H. Hansen of Minnesota University for recent information concerning unemployment and wages, and W. L. Crum of Yale University for helpful suggestions regarding the statistical treatment. To Professor W. C. Mitchell the author is extremely grateful for the many helpful suggestions and criticisms he made after reading the manuscript, and finally he is indebted especially to Professor H. R. Seager, under whose critical supervision the treatise has been written.

CONTENTS

CHAPTER I

GENERAL SURVEY

THE American Labor Movement has been defined in various ways by those who have written concerning it. As used in this monograph, it is another name for the continuous attempts of organized labor in America to realize its desires and demands. The term is limited here to organized labor because there are no authentic data available relating to the desires and demands of unorganized labor. The attitude and programs of the American Federation of Labor and the Amalgamated Clothing Workers of America are taken as representative of the attitude and ideas of organized labor in general, because, in the first place, the majority of organized workers are connected in some way with one or the other of these organizations; and in the second place, reliable and consecutive data concerning labor organizations outside these two are not available. It may be said that the aim of organized labor as represented by the American Federation of Labor and the Amalgamated Clothing Workers of America appears to be to "improve the status of the wage-earning classes by promoting an opportunistic or practical program of reform".

A business cycle may be defined as a succession of events completed during the interval between a given point of time in a period of prosperity or depression, and a corresponding point of time in the succeeding period of prosperity or depression. Some writers consider the period from 1915 to 1922 as a complete cycle, but according to our definition of a business cycle, this period includes more than one cycle. There was not an unbroken upward trend of the business curve during the period of prosperity; for example, there was a recession in business activity in the latter part of 1917, and 1918 was still more a period of declining profits. Further, there was a distinct reaction from activity after the Armistice. In other words, the latter part of 1916 or the first part of 1917 marked the peak of prosperity following the depression of 1914 and the revival of 1915.

The upward swing of the business curve in the second half of 1919 and the peak of prosperity in 1920, may be regarded as parts of a new cycle marked off from the war cycle by the brief period of depression in the first quarter of 1919.

Entrepreneurs had prepared for falling prices after the Armistice, and were taken by surprise when the great post-war buying campaign developed in the early summer. To take advantage of the situation, they marked up prices and expanded the scale of operations as rapidly as possible. The latter part of 1919 seemed, therefore, to be a period of extraordinary activity, arising from unusual conditions created by the war. We shall consider the period between 1915 and 1922, then, as including two business cycles.

The year 1913 was a time of slowly shrinking activity both in Europe and America. The depression had become pronounced early in 1914 and the outbreak of the war added financial confusion and uncertainty to the difficulties with which business men had to contend. The winter of 1914-15 was a period of severe unemployment in the United States, and the revival of activity produced by huge European orders did not make much headway until the middle of 1915.

The year 1915, therefore, marks the beginning of the period of prosperity, which lasted, except for the qualifications already mentioned, until the Armistice.

A great depression began in the first quarter of 1920 and did not reach its lowest ebb until the middle of 1921, at which time business conditions began to improve. While slow at first, the improvement gathered momentum as the months passed, until by the end of 1922 conditions had become "normal" in many respects.

The general trend of business conditions can be more readily visualized by aid of a curve. The chart on page 16 shows the changing conditions of business, month by month, from 1915 to 1922, and probably gives a trustworthy picture of the general trend during the whole period.

Various methods have been used in an effort to compile a satisfactory business index from such data as the statistics of physical production, railway tonnage, bank clearings, etc. One of the most widely used indices of business conditions is that computed by the Harvard Committee on Economic Research. The figures for this curve of business conditions are compiled from *Bradstreet's* price index and *Bradstreet's* bank clearings outside of New York City,[1] which according to Professor W. C. Mitchell, who made a test of the seven leading American index numbers of prices, gives the best index of business conditions.[2] "The fact that *Bradstreet's* publishes the actual prices entering the index and describes its method of construction, gives one confidence in using the index." [3]

The Harvard Committee, in working out this index of business conditions, found that such items as average prices

[1] See the files of the *Review of Economic Statistics.* Data for bank clearings are monthly averages, and *Bradstreet's* prices relate to the first day of the month. See also the files of Bradstreet's, and the *Commercial and Financial Chronicle.*

[2] See *Bulletin No. 284* of the Bureau of Labor Statistics, p. 111.

[3] W. M. Persons, "An Index of General Business Conditions," *Review of Economic Statistics,* April, 1919, p. 141. For a list of the particular articles included in the index, see pp. 140-141.

of railway bonds, industrial stocks, railroad stocks, volume of sales on the New York Stock Exchange, and New York clearings, all fluctuated readily upward or downward, depending upon speculation. These items were plotted as a separate group and called the speculative group, since they were found to be best suited for an index of speculation. It was also found that the series of items in which the fluctuations tended to lag behind the fluctuations of the speculative group, all had to do with business and industrial activity, and constituted the business group. This group was found to include "pig-iron production, bank clearings outside of New York City, *Bradstreet's* indices of commodity prices, and the index of commodity prices of the Bureau of Labor Statistics". There was a third series of items, which constituted the banking group, whose fluctuations lagged behind the business group. This third group included "rates on commercial paper, and loans, deposits, and reserves of New York banks".[1] The business group was chosen because it reflected the changes in business conditions and industrial activity more accurately than the items in the other two groups.

It was found that after the outbreak of the war in 1914 some of the items in the business group lost their value as an index of business conditions and developments. This was due to the abnormal economic conditions, the influence of government control in industry, and changes in economic organization, which caused violent and erratic fluctuations in the "statistical series", as well as "an abrupt break in the continuity of the phenomena which they measure and reflect". Because of these difficulties, bank clearings outside of New York City and *Bradstreet's* commodity prices seemed best adapted to the business group.

[1] W. M. Persons, "A Non-technical Explanation of the Index of General Business Conditions", *Review of Economic Statistics*, February, 1920, p. 41.

The statistical department of the American Telephone and Telegraph Company computed an index of business conditions by the same method as that used by the Harvard Committee,[1] but since 1922 the index has been based upon items representing physical quantities.[2] Since the beginning of this index

there have been successive additions of new series, accompanied by an elimination of a smaller number of the older and less satisfactory series. The reliability of the curve is, therefore, somewhat greater in recent than in earlier years. Since April, 1922, 'bank clearings' and 'debits to individual accounts' have been dropped, owing to the difficulty experienced in adjusting for price changes, and the index is now based wholly on items representing physical quantities.[3]

Each of the series was analyzed separately and corrected for seasonal variation and long-term trend.[4] This index is chosen in preference to the Harvard index because it is based primarily upon physical production, and therefore should bear a close relationship to the employment index. Table I gives the figures from which the curve of business conditions was plotted.

[1] See *Review of Economic Statistics*, vol. i, 1919, *passim*.

[2] The items from which the index numbers after April 1922 were computed, together with their relative weights are as follows: production of pig iron (wt. 20), unfilled orders of the United States Steel Corporation, freight car demand, cotton consumption, activity wool machinery, and paper production were each given a weight of 10. Car loading, net freight ton miles, production of coal, lumber production, leather production, and power production were given a weight of 5 each.

[3] See M. C. Rorty, "The Statistical Control of Business Activities," *Harvard Business Review*, January, 1923, p. 160.

[4] The year 1916 was used by the Harvard Committee as the "terminal year of the period" for determining secular trend. The secular trend for the period following 1916 was determined by extending the "straight lines determined from the data of the preceding period,

TABLE I

COMPOSITE INDEX OF GENERAL BUSINESS ACTIVITY [1]

(Figures indicate percentage deviations from normal)

Month	1915	1916	1917	1918	1919	1920	1921	1922
January	−16	+11	+17	+ 4	+4	+13	−19	−16
February	−13	+12	+13	+ 3	−3	+10	−18	−11
March	−12	+13	+14	+10	−8	+12	−22	−10
April	− 9	+ 9	+12	+10	−6	+ 9	−25	−16
May	− 8	+12	+14	+13	−2	+ 6	−25	−14
June	− 4	+11	+12	+10	+0	+ 8	−23	−11
July	− 3	+ 8	+10	+14	+7	+ 8	−25	−12
August	− 2	+12	+10	+15	+9	+ 7	−21	−10
September	+ 2	+13	+ 7	+11	+8	+ 5	−19	− 6
October	+ 5	+15	+ 9	+10	+7	− 1	−18	− 2
November	+ 9	+17	+11	+ 5	+4	− 6	−15	....
December	+14	+16	+ 6	+ 6	+8	−11	−14	....

The purpose of the curve of business conditions is to give a graphic picture of the general trend of business from 1915 to 1922 inclusive, in order that the relation between business conditions and the volume of employment, labor mobility, cost of living, membership of organized labor, etc., can be seen more easily. In other words, an explanation of the influence of the business cycle on the American labor movement is facilitated by graphic and tabular presentation of these social phenomena. This curve shows a general upward trend until the end of 1916. During 1917, it fell below the level for the previous year, but after 1917, it shows a rapid revival until September of 1918, at which time it falls decidedly, due largely to the feeling that the

1903-1916." This was done because it is doubtful if the changes brought about by conditions after our entrance into the war are in the "nature of a change of trend." A discussion of this point can be found in the *Review of Economic Statistics*, vol. i, p. 39.

[1] M. C. Rorty, *loc. cit.*, p. 159.

war would soon end. The rise of the curve in 1919 reflects the revival after the Armistice, which revival continued until the first part of 1920. In the Spring of 1920, the curve shows a decline, slow at first, and then quite rapid until the middle of 1921, when the trough of the depression was reached. After July, 1921, the curve rises rather rapidly, showing the revival of business conditions that followed the depression. The break in the latter part of 1918 shows the effect of the general feeling among the captains of industry that a period of deflation and falling prices would follow the signing of the Armistice. The influence of the Armistice became manifest even before it was actually signed, for the industrial leaders anticipated and prepared to meet the industrial changes that they felt would inevitably result. The decline in the latter part of 1919 was due to the steel and coal strikes while the break in April, 1922, shows the effect of the coal strikes of that date. The curve also reflects the influence of the railroad shop men's strike which began in July, 1922. The upward swings of the curve during the latter part of 1921, and all of 1922 are greater than the downward tendencies, so that the general trend of the curve is decidedly upward.

An attempt is made in this monograph to show how changes in wages, prices, employment, labor mobility, labor absenteeism, etc., during the years 1915-1922 tended to emphasize the effect of business prosperity on the attitude of organized wage earners. To measure the effect accurately is impossible, for at the same time that business conditions are exerting an influence on these different phenomena, several other factors and conditions are also exercising their influence. This was especially true of these years because coincident with them came the increasing influence of workers' education on social conditions, a drastic restriction of immigration, and the war itself with its profound

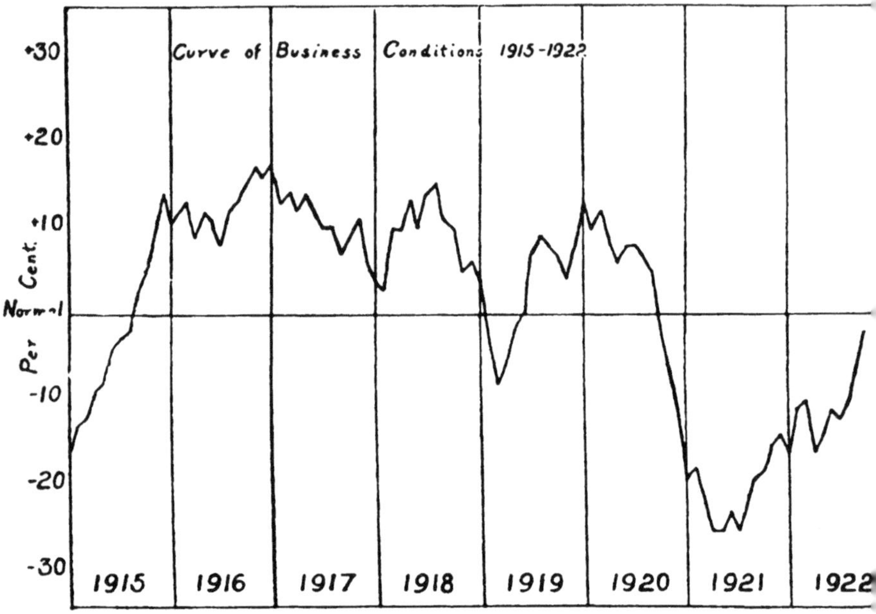

effect upon individual psychology. In studying economic statistics and problems of this kind, we are not able to segregate or control these outside and interacting influences, and we are, therefore, usually compelled to give conclusions in terms of general trends rather than in more precise terms. Despite the fact that we cannot measure the effect of business conditions upon wages, prices, employment, labor mobility and absenteeism, it has been shown rather conclusively by Professor W. F. Ogburn and others, that business cycles do have a very direct effect upon these various social phenomena, and that their combined influence, in turn, shapes and molds the character of the labor movement.

It is quite generally believed that when wages are rising more slowly than prices, wage earners will take the offensive in an effort to maintain their real wages, which in turn means that the labor movement will in such periods be more violent and aggressive in character; on the other hand, when prices are falling faster than wages, employers take the offensive and wage earners will fight to keep their money wages from falling. But in general, it is held that the efforts of the wage earners are more successful during periods of prosperity when prices are rising than during periods of falling prices when they are acting on the defensive.

Another idea was advanced during the last period of prosperity by many of the more conservative employers, namely, that organization of the workers does not tend to raise the wages of the laborers. This, they claimed, was shown by the fact that during the war, wages of the more strongly organized workers increased less than wages in industries where the workers were less strongly organized.

As to employment, it has been claimed that during periods of prosperity when there is a place open to everyone in industry and there is very little unemployment, laborers will take the offensive and the labor movement will assume quite a different character from that which it assumes during periods of depression, when workers are desirous of maintaining the *status quo*. In the next place, many believe that labor absenteeism and mobility, both of which increase during periods of prosperity, mean more freedom, liberty, and leisure for the working classes, which are immediately reflected in the labor movement by demands for shorter hours, better conditions, and more control.

It is also the generally accepted opinion that industrial conditions between 1915 and 1920 were such that the wage-earners were able to gain concessions from their employers which they never before had been able to realize, and that the great increase in the demand for products, resulting from the exhaustion of the supplies and resources of the European countries, and also our entrance into the war, eliminated the problems of marketing. This opinion is based upon the idea that the producers or employers were not confronted with the difficulties of marketing their products at a profit, but rather with the problem of maintaining a sufficient supply of labor and equipment to supply the already existing demand.

These various opinions were often based upon "common knowledge" and had no scientifically reliable foundation. It is my purpose in the following chapters to analyse the interacting influences of the various phases of the business cycle, such as the closely interrelated problems of wages, cost of living and unemployment, which in turn give rise to the other phases, labor mobility and absenteeism, all of which influence, more or less directly, the character of the labor movement. An attempt is made to show statistically, by means of both tabular and graphic presentation, the extent to which the various opinions and theories mentioned are borne out by the facts. In many cases, the statistics are incomplete, because of the paucity of reliable data, but in such instances an effort has been made to indicate the source of the data and to point out their incompleteness.

The successful prosecution of the war necessitated a continuous and efficient labor supply for the production of war materials. Soon after our entrance into the war, we were faced with the necessity of changing many manufacturing plants from producing peace-time articles to the production of articles necessary in time of war. Increased production was more than offset by increased foreign and domestic demand, and prices thus continued to rise higher and higher as more gold flowed into the country and inflation set in. High prices and increased volume of trade stimulated employers to make every effort to maintain an adequate supply of labor, in order to realize the large profit resulting therefrom. The problem was complicated still more by the drafting of great numbers of laborers into military service.

The workers were not long in realizing their potential power and in taking advantage of the situation. They flocked to the shipbuilding and other industrial centers where the government was letting large contracts for work of various kinds. Many of these contracts were let on a cost plus basis, and consequently, contractors were willing to pay almost any wage demanded, for the more it cost to complete the contract, the more profit the employer made. Contractors were bidding against each other for laborers and this caused the workers to be changing constantly from one employer to another for a slightly higher wage. Manufacturers without such contracts could not compete with the wages being paid by these contracting employers. Mr. Bing describes the situation as follows:

After our entrance into the war the Government awarded contracts on cost plus basis. War psychology, as well as the demand of Government departments, laid emphasis on speed rather than economy. Contractors and Government officials, in their eagerness to get their particular pieces of work done, disregarded the effect of their actions on other Government work, and the stealing of men from one plant to another was freely indulged in, Government departments and employers bidding against each other for men and supplies. Many firms, when they wanted men, showed themselves absolutely unscrupulous in the manner in which they disregarded the wishes and even the express orders of Government officials regarding wages and overtime.[1]

Professor L. C. Marshall tells of one "community in which an investigator met incoming trains and watched workers accept employment in as many as six to ten plants in the

[1] A. M. Bing, *War-Time Strikes and their Adjustment*, (New York, 1921), p. 8.

same day, moving from one to the other in the hope of ever-higher wages and accepting employment in every one whose wage offer was larger than that of its predecessor." [1]

It was conditions of this kind that emphasized the importance and seriousness of the problems of wages, employment, cost of living, labor mobility and absenteeism, and that caused the government to make special studies of the existing situation and to create various adjustment and administrative agencies for handling the many problems that resulted from war conditions.

[1] L. C. Marshall, "The War Labor Program", *Journal of Political Economy*, 1918, p. 429.

CHAPTER II

Wages and the Cost of Living

The Bureau of Labor Statistics has published from time to time index numbers of the cost of living. During the period of rising prices, surveys of several hundred families were made in each community studied by the Bureau, in order to obtain a reliable index.[1] The relative importance of each article in the family budget was determined, together with the local retail prices of the various articles entering into the budget. The National Industrial Conference Board used similar methods of weighting, and used the figures of the Bureau of Labor Statistics for the retail price of food. Most of the other prices were obtained by correspondence.[2] Table II, which follows, shows the per cent increase in cost of living according to budget items, as published by the Bureau of Labor Statistics.

The National Industrial Conference Board found that the cost of living increased approximately ninety-five per cent. between July, 1914, and March, 1920. This estimate is a little more conservative than that of the Bureau of Labor Statistics. This is probably due to the difference in methods used. The National Industrial Conference Board gathered many

[1] See *Monthly Labor Review*, Oct., 1919, pp. 1-8.

[2] See *Report No. 49* of the National Industrial Conference Board, April, 1922, pp. 30 and 31, for a table of the increase in cost of living by budget items between July, 1914, and March, 1922. The Board has also published *Research Reports Numbers 20, 31, 35,* and *45* on changes in wages in the United States.

TABLE II

Changes in the Cost of Living in the United States [1]

Budget Item	Per cent of total expenditure	Per cent Increase from 1913 (average) to Dec., 1914	Dec., 1915	Dec., 1916	Dec., 1917	Dec., 1918	June, 1919	Dec., 1919	June, 1920	Dec., 1920	May, 1921	Dec., 1921	March, 1922	June, 1922	Dec., 1922
Food	38.2	5.0	5.0	26.0	57.0	87.0	84.0	97.0	119.0	78.0	44.7	49.9	38.7	41.0	46.6
Clothing	16.6	1.0	4.7	20.0	49.1	105.3	114.5	168.7	187.5	158.5	122.6	84.4	75.5	72.3	71.5
Housing	13.4	([2])	1.5	2.3	.1	9.2	14.2	25.3	34.9	51.1	59.0	61.4	60.9	60.9	61.9
Fuel and light	5.3	1.0	1.0	8.4	24.1	47.9	45.6	56.8	71.9	94.9	81.6	81.1	75.8	74.2	86.4
Furniture and furnishings	5.1	4.0	10.6	27.8	50.6	113.6	125.1	163.5	192.7	185.4	147.7	118.0	106.2	102.9	108.2
Miscellaneous	21.3	3.0	7.4	13.3	40.5	65.8	73.2	90.2	101.4	108.2	108.8	106.8	103.3	101.1	100.5
Total	100.0	3.0	5.1	18.3	42.4	74.4	77.3	99.3	116.5	100.4	80.4	74.3	66.9	66.6	69.5

[1] See *Monthly Labor Review*, July, 1921, p. 112, May, 1922, p. 76, and May, 1923, p. 100,

[2] No change.

of its price and rent data "by correspondence with clothing stores, real estate dealers," etc., and the error due to this method of collecting data would naturally be on the conservative side, since the interests of the two latter, and their fear of being accused of profiteering, would cause them to give minimum prices.

The percentages for the cost of living, as given in Table II, do not reflect changes as accurately as they would if they were given for each month, but absence of monthly data is partly compensated by the fact that figures are given for the middle of 1919, 1920 and 1921. The table shows that the cost of living reached its highest point in June, 1920, at which time the index number was 116.5 per cent higher than the 1913 average. In December, 1920, the index number was only 100.4 per cent higher than in 1913. Since, therefore, we have mid-year figures for the year that prices ceased rising and began to fall, as well as for the year preceding and following the beginning of the decline of prices, the indices give a reasonably complete picture of the general trend of cost of living.

In addition to the cost-of-living indices, the Bureau of Labor Statistics has published figures of the union scale of wages in the United States from 1907 to date. The index numbers of these rates are based on the "union minimum rates" according to the agreements between employers and employees. In many cases men were paid, by individual agreement, higher wages than the union scale specified; therefore, the union rate is somewhat lower than the average actual wage. Actual wage is used here in the sense of total money wage, and includes in addition to the union wage, payment for overtime, bonuses, and extra pay for special skill. The union wage figures are not averages, but are given for May of each year. The following table shows the trend of hourly wages together with the changes in cost of living:

TABLE III

INDEX NUMBERS OF HOURLY WAGES, AND COST OF LIVING, 1915-1922 [1]

1916 = 100

Year	Union Hourly Rates	Actual Hourly Earnings [2]	Changes in Cost of Living [3]
1915	96.2	92.8	88.8
1916	100.0	100 0	100.0
1917	106.5	126.4	120.3
1918	124.3	151.1	142.4
1919	144.8	179.9	168.4
1920	185.9	217.2	177.8
1921	191.6	188.6	147.3
1922	180.4	179.6	143.3

The number of trades and occupations covered in the reports from which the union or minimum wage figures were compiled varies, but includes in general about twelve industries with from three to twenty-seven trades in each industry.[4] The information was taken from sixty-six cities located in thirty-six different states.

[1] For index numbers of union wages from 1913 to 1921, see *Monthly Labor Review*, Dec., 1921, p. 90, and *Bulletin 302* of the Bureau of Labor Statistics.

[2] Except in case of Navy Yards, for which hourly wages are used, the figures for actual hourly earnings are taken from hourly earnings in the following industries: iron and steel, railways, boot and shoe, cotton goods manufacturing, woolen and worsted goods, and navy yards. The data for the boot and shoe, cotton goods, woolen and worsted goods, and iron and steel industries were compiled from the wage figures published by the Bureau of Labor Statistics, the wage figures for the railway industry were compiled from the reports of the Interstate Commerce Commission, and those for the Navy Yards were taken from the records of the Navy Department.

[3] Figures for December. The index numbers for June, 1919, 1920, and 1922, are 149.7, 183.0 and 140.8 respectively. The May, 1921, index is 152.4 and the March and September, 1922, indices are 141.1 and 140.5 respectively.

[4] Following is a list of the industries included in the May, 1920 Report: bakery trades; building trades; chauffeurs, teamsters, and drivers;

The Bureau defines the union scale as a statement, "either written or definitely understood, of wages and hours of labor agreed to or accepted by an organization of union men and an employer or group of employers, under which agreement, expressed or implied, union men actually work."[1] The union scale sets a minimum wage and maximum hours for a day's work. Bonuses were included in the general union rate when all received bonuses, but when only a few or special ones received bonuses they were mentioned in a footnote.

The changes in actual wages of workers is shown by the following table of wages compiled from information gathered from pay-rolls in six of the larger industries. This table also includes some of the industries from which union rates were figured.

The figures in Table IV represent average hourly earnings for all of the industries given, except in case of the navy yards, where wages are given in terms of hourly rates. Average hourly earnings were computed by dividing the total earnings for the pay-roll period by the total number of hours worked during the period.[2] The hourly rates merely give what is earned per hour for each hour that is actually worked, and are, therefore, not affected by overtime and unemployment on the part of the workers.

freight handlers; granite and stone trade cutters; laundry workers; metal workes; mill work; printing and publishing (book job); printing and publishing (newspaper); theatrical employees; and waiters. The Bureau of Labor Statistics has published eight bulletins, previously to this, on union scale of wages and hours of labor. *Bulletin No. 131* covers data from 1907 to 1912, *No. 143* includes data for 1913, *No. 171* for 1914, *No. 194* for 1915, *No. 214* for 1916, *No. 245* for 1917, *No. 259* for 1918, *No. 274* for 1919, and *No. 286* for 1920.

[1] See *Bulletin No. 245*, p. 10, of the Bureau of Labor Statistics.

[2] See *Monthly Labor Review*, January, 1920, p. 122.

TABLE IV

AVERAGE HOURLY EARNINGS IN SIX LEADING INDUSTRIES[1]

Industry	1915	1916	1917	1918	1919	1920	1921	1922
Woolen and worsted goods	$.205	$.221	......	$.329	......	$.577	......	$.450
Boot and shoe[2]	.313	.322	......	.473	......	.541	......	.499
Cotten goods manufacturing	.160	.187	......	.276	......	.492	......	.349
Railways	.347	.355	$.399	.588	$.630	.783	$.728	.724[3]
Navy yards[4]	.457	.475	.578	.697	.776	.776	.818	.708
Iron and steel	.358	.408[5]	.592	......	.813	.929	......	......

The data for the boot and shoe industry are given in the September, 1922, Monthly Labor Review.[6] The number of

[1] The corresponding index numbers showing average increase is given in Table VIII.

[2] The 1915 figures for boot and shoe, cotton goods, and woolen and worsted goods are computed on the assumption of a uniform increase between 1914 and 1916.

[3] Unweighted average for all employees in 1922, other than executives, officials and clerks. The averages for 1915 to June, 1921, inclusive are weighted according to the number of employees in June, 1919.

[4] Hourly rates computed from daily rates on the basis of the eight hour day.

[5] Average estimated on the basis of per capita increase in 1916 over 1915. The Bureau of Labor Statistics publishes in the *Monthly Labor Review* monthly figures of the total amount of the pay-roll and the number of persons on the pay-roll for various industries. The average per capita increase in 1916 over 1915 was computed from these figures for iron and steel.

[6] The Bureau has published the following reports on wages and hours of labor in the boot and shoe industry: *Nineteenth Annual Report*, covering 1890 to 1903; *Bulletin No. 59*, covering 1903 and 1904; *No. 65*, covering 1904 and 1905; *No. 71*, covering 1905 and 1906; *No. 77*, covering 1906 and 1907; *No. 134*, covering 1907 to 1912; *No. 154*, covering 1912 and 1913; *No. 178*, covering 1913 and 1914; *No. 232*, covering 1914 and 1916; *No. 260*, covering 1916 and 1918; and *No. 278*, covering 1920 with a summary for years 1907 to 1918 inclusive. See also *Monthly Labor Review*, Aug., 1920, pp. 74-81.

establishments furnishing data, and the number of employees included in the survey, varied from year to year, but not enough to invalidate the figures for purposes of comparison. The figures for 1922, included 47,361 employees, and 104 representative factories located in 13 states. The majority of the data were taken from the April and May pay-rolls.

Information regarding wages and hours of labor in the cotton-goods manufacturing industry is given in *Bulletin 288* of the Bureau of Labor Statistics for the years 1907-1920. Data were not collected for the years 1915, 1917, 1919, and 1921.[1] The 1922 average was computed by taking the average of the figures for Massachusetts and for the Southern States and weighting them according to the number of persons employed. In 1922, the Massachusetts survey included 16,380 employees, and in the Southern States, 29,759 employees were included. The number of establishments covered for the various years in the country at large was as follows: 105 in 1916, 106 in 1918, 96 in 1920, and 57 in 1922.

The wage data for woolen and worsted goods were taken from the pay-rolls of representative establishments, by the agents of the Bureau, in practically the same way that the information for the boot and shoe, and cotton manufacturing industries was gathered. The number of establishments covered was as follows: 61 in 1916, 63 in 1918, 67 in 1920,

[1] The Bureau has published previous reports of wages and hours of labor in cotton-goods manufacturing, as follows: *Nineteenth Annual Report*, covering the years 1890-1893; *Bulletin No. 59*, covering 1903-1904; *No. 65*, covering 1904-1905; *No. 71*, covering 1905-1906; *No. 77*, covering 1906-1907; *No. 128*, covering 1907-1912; *No. 150*, covering 1912-1913; *No. 190*, covering 1913-1914; *No. 239*, covering 1914-1916; *No. 262*, covering 1916-1918. The *Monthly Labor Review* for May, 1922, pp. 100-105 gives information for the State of Massachusetts from 1907 to 1922, and the Sept., 1922, number covers the cotton-manufacturing industry in the Southern States from 1907-1922.

and 67 in 1922. No data were gathered for 1915, 1917, 1919, and 1921. A summary of the wages and hours of labor in the woolen and worsted industry from 1907 to 1922 is given in the October, 1922, *Monthly Labor Review*.[1]

The majority of the wage data for the navy yards were taken from twelve representative navy yards, and represent fifteen selected occupations. Figures for 1920 and 1921 were taken from the East and West coasts without the number of yards being designated. The 1920 rates were those which were in effect from November 9, 1918, to September 15, 1920. Those for 1921 resulted from the September 16, 1920, agreement, and continued until September 15, 1921. The wage rates for 1922 were the result of the September 16, 1921, agreement and are still in force. The schedules of wage rates in the Navy Department have not been published, but these figures were compiled from the records of the Department.[2] The following table gives the wage rates for various occupations:[3]

[1] Previous reports on wages and hours of labor in the woolen and worsted industry are as follows: *Nineteenth Annual Report*, covering 1890-1903; *Bulletin No. 59*, covering 1903 and 1904; *No. 65*, covering 1904 and 1905; *No. 71*, covering 1905 and 1906; *No. 77*, covering 1906 and 1907; *No. 128*, covering 1907 to 1912; *No. 150*, covering 1912 and 1913; *No. 190*, covering 1914 and 1915; *No. 238*, covering 1914 and 1916; *No. 261*, covering 1916 and 1918; and *No. 289*, covering 1920. See also *Monthly Labor Review*, Mar., 1921, pp. 67-69.

[2] The wages paid in the navy yards were included because of the paucity of wage data for other industries. It would have been better to have included wages, for example, in the meat-packing industry or coal mining, but information is given for only two years in these industries.

[3] In determining the earnings of the workers, weighted averages were used when information relative to the number of wage-earners was available. Otherwise unweighted averages were used.

TABLE V

DAILY WAGE RATES FOR SELECTED OCCUPATIONS IN THE NAVY YARDS

Occupation	1915	1916	1917	1918	1919	1920	1921	1922
Boiler makers	$3.73	$3.87	$4.86	$5.66	$6.40	$6.40	....	$5.84
Copper smiths	3.97	4.06	4.97	5.94	6.88	6.88	$7.20	6.24
Electricians	4.13	4.20	4.82	5.64	6.40	6.40	6.72	5.84
Machinists	3.83	4.09	4.87	5.81	6.40	6.40	6.72	5.84
Machinists (electrical)	3.8[illegible]	4.07	4.85	5.83	6.40	6.40	6.72	....
Molders	3.85	4.04	4.86	5.81	6.40	6.40	7.20	6.24
Pattern makers	4.16	4.23	5.08	6.25	6.98	6.98	....	6.64
Pipe fitters	3.73	3.85	4.87	5.81	6.40	6.40	....	5.84
Plumbers	4.07	4.17	4.84	5.81	6.40	6.40	6.72	5.84
Riveters	3.48	3.56	4.79	5.65	6.40	6.40	6.72	5.84
Shipfitters	3.80	4.03	4.90	5.82	6.40	6.40	6.72	5.84
Shipsmiths	3.83	3.92	4.83	5.81	6.40	6.40	6.72	5.84
Toolmakers	3.95	4.15	4.93	6.24	6.88	6.88	....	6.24
Holders on	2.46	2.65	3.39	4.16	4.85	4.85	....	4.24
Laborers (common)	2.03	2.09	2.57	3.07	3.56	3.56	4.12	3.12
Average	$3.66	$3.80	$4.63	$5.55	$6.21	$6.21	$6.55	$5.67

It is interesting to note how in 1919, 1920, and 1921, the rates for various occupations tended to uniformity, many of the different classes receiving exactly the same wage. This is a good illustration of the way in which the adjustment agencies affected the wage rates for various classes of workers.

The figures for wages of the railway workers were compiled from *Statistics of Railways in the United States* and from quarterly and monthly reports of the Interstate Commerce Commission, Bureau of Statistics. The following table shows the average compensation received by various classes of employees on Class I railways:

TABLE VI

HOURLY WAGE RATES FOR SELECTED OCCUPATIONS ON CLASS I RAILWAYS IN THE UNITED STATES, 1915-1922

Occupation	1915	1916	1917	1918	1919	1920	1921	1922
Machinists	$ .397	$ .410	$ .462	$ .728	$ .745	$ .835	$ .880	......
Boilermakers	.398	.409	.462	.724	.752	.847	.895	......
Painters and upholsterers	.301	.309	.347	.558	.667	.747	.818	......
Other unskilled labor	.186	.194	.224	.336	.426	.575	.630	......
Other construction and work-train labor	.169	.181	.206	.310	.405	.493	.525	......
Hostlers	.256	.259	.311	.484	.571	.469	.483	......
Road freight engineers and motormen	.608	.610	.691	.812	.922	.628	.673	......
Road freight firemen and helpers	.380	.391	.447	.595	.677	.640	.680	......
Road freight conductors	.502	.500	.564	.694	.763	.657	.730	......
Road passenger engineers and motormen	.904	.899	.914	.992	1.168	1.100	1.156	......
Road passenger firemen and helpers	.561	.560	.569	.705	.855	.824	.877	......
Road passenger conductors	.715	.710	.737	.848	.970	.698	.975	......
Telegraphers, telephoners, and block operators	.272	.282	.310	.430	.578	1.214	1.365	......
Telegraphers, telephoners, and operating interlockers	.291	.302	.323	.444	.597	.965	1.052	......
Mechanics' helpers and apprentices	.230	.238	.276	.453	.490	1.051	1.145	......
Average	$ .347	$ .355	$ .399	$ .588	.630	.783	.871[1]	.695

The figures for the years 1915 to 1918 can be found in the *Statistics of Railways in the United States*, and figures for 1919, 1920, and the first half of 1921 are given in quarterly reports of The Interstate Commerce Commission in a little different form from those given in previous reports. Beginning July 1, 1921, monthly summary reports

[1] This is the average for the first half of 1921. The average for the entire year of 1921 is .728. The averages for 1915 to June 1921 inclusive are weighted according to the number of employees in June, 1919. The 1921 average was computed by averaging the averages for the first and last half of the year.

were started as a result of an order issued by the Interstate Commerce Commission April 18, 1921, and effective July 1. These reports are different from any previous ones and, therefore, comparisons of the old and new figures must be made with care. The Bureau of Statistics of the Interstate Commerce Commission gives the reason for the last change as follows:

The new wage statistics were designed to meet the needs of both the United States Railroad Labor Board and the Interstate Commerce Commission. The number of reporting divisions or classes has been increased from 66 to 148, and an analysis of the hours of service and compensation has been introduced. The increased number of classes does not result from a mere subdivision of the classes used in the old form, but is the out-growth of an exhaustive classification study conducted by the United States Railroad Labor Board.

The difference in the method of reporting makes it impossible to give detailed information for each of the occupations or classes after July, 1921, in the same form as information for previous years is given, because the same classes are not carried through all of the years. For example, data for the first half of 1921 are given in the same way as they were reported in 1919 and 1920, but figures for the last half are given in a different form; therefore, detailed data for the last part of 1921, and for 1922 can not be given in the same form as they are for the previous years. In computing the average for 1922 it was necessary to take an average of the wage rates for the groups as a whole, rather than for each occupation. The same method was used in computing the average for the last half of 1921. This difference in methods used in computing the averages, however, has very little effect on the average wage for the industry as a whole, which after all is the thing that interests us primarily.

Wage data for the iron and steel industry were obtained through personal visits of agents of the Bureau of Labor Statistics, and by correspondence with the plants. Ten departments of the industry were represented. It was the purpose of the Bureau, in the 1920 survey, to obtain data when the wage rates were at the highest point, but in some cases reductions had been made prior to the survey. Earnings per hour were figured in the same way as they were for the other industries.[1] The average hourly earnings for each department are given in the following table:

TABLE VII

AVERAGE HOURLY EARNINGS IN IRON AND STEEL INDUSTRY, 1915 TO 1920[2]

Department	1915	1917	1919	1920
Blast furnaces	$.210	$.314	$.514	$.586
Bessemer converters.	.350	.588	.805	.919
Open hearth	.270	.405	.637	.727
Puddling mills.....	.335	....	.908	1.036
Blooming mills	.392	.555	.827	.880
Plate mills	.388	.549	.877	.910
Standard rail mills..	.304	....	.656	.797
Bar mills..........	.329	....	.741	.824
Sheet mills........	.543	1.140	1.129	1.422
Tin plate mills.....	.462	....	1.037	1.191
Average	$.358	$.592	$.813	$.929

[1] *Cf. supra*, pp. 17-18.

[2] Detailed data for 1916 are not available. See *Bulletin no. 305* of the Bureau of Labor Statistics, "Wages and Hours of Labor in the Iron and Steel Industry: 1907 to 1920". Previous reports on wages and hours of labor in iron and steel are as follows: *Bulletin no. 218* covers the years up to 1915; *Monthly Labor Review*, for Mar., 1918, pp. 41-51 covers 1917; and *Bulletin no. 265* covers 1919.

The index numbers of the actual hourly earnings for the six industries given in Table IV are as follows:

TABLE VIII

INDEX NUMBERS OF WAGES IN SIX LEADING INDUSTRIES [1]

1916 = 100

Industry	1915	1916	1918	1920	1922
Woolen and worsted goods...	92.7	100	148.8	261.0	203 6
Boot and shoe...............	97.2	100	146.9	168.0	154 9
Cotton goods manufacturing ..	85.5	100	147.5	263.1	186.6
Railways	97.7	100	165.6	220.6	203.9
Navy Yards	96.2	100	146 7	163.3	149.0
Iron and steel	87.7	100 [2]	....	227.6	....
Average	92.8	100	151.1	217.2	179 6

A graphic presentation of the relation between wages and cost of living is given in the chart on p. 25. As can be seen from the chart, the cost-of-living curve remained above the union wage curve during 1917, 1918 and 1919. The union hourly wages are higher than the weekly wages because of changes in the number of hours worked; therefore, if the curve of union weekly wages were plotted, it would be below the hourly wage curve. In cases where hours were reduced in number, the full-time weekly earnings fell below the hourly rates, because weekly earnings are computed by multiplying the hourly rates by the number of hours per week. When the hours worked per week are reduced, the weekly wages are necessarily decreased. The aotual wage,

[1] Wage data for 1917, 1919 and 1921 are available for only the railway industry and navy yards. The average index number for these industries is 126.4 in 1917, 179.9 in 1919 and 188.6 in 1921. These averages are not plotted because they are not sufficiently representative of general wage rates.

[2] *Cf. supra*, p. 11.

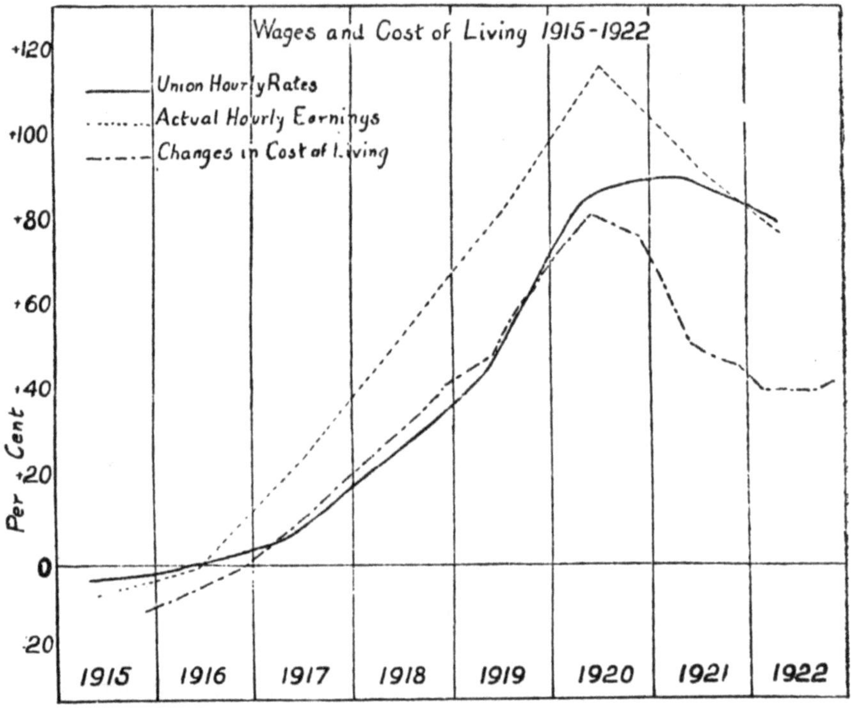

based upon average hourly earnings, was much higher than the union or minimum hourly rates, because of special individual wage agreements, bonuses, and overtime, which were not included in the union wages. The difference between the two wage curves may also be due in part to the fact that union rates are based upon annual data taken for May of each year, while the actual wage curve is based upon average hourly earnings taken from various pay-roll periods during the year.[1]

[1] The figures for union wages, hourly earnings, and cost of living are not strictly comparable since they were taken at different periods of the year. The curves, therefore, should be used only as indicating general trends.

There is another limitation on the accuracy of the data of actual wages, due to the fact that information was gathered for different pay-roll periods for the different industries, and even for the different establishments of the same industry. These various limitations and qualifications on the use of the actual wage data, therefore, make it impossible to draw definite conclusions. The most that we can do is to use the information as an index of the general trend or tendency of actual wages. In this respect, however, it seems that the curve of actual earnings should show the relation between wages and cost of living more accurately, during the last period of prosperity, than the union rates do, because of the influence of overtime, bonuses, and special agreements. What we are interested in, is determining as nearly as possible just what the real wages of labor were during the period under consideration, rather than what the wages would have been, had all the workers been receiving the union or minimum wage. Data taken from the pay-rolls of the various concerns and covering thousands of individuals, should give us more accurate results for this purpose than union rates.

Wage data should be based upon annual income rather than hourly rates or earnings, in order that accurate comparisons may be made with the cost-of-living figures, and definite conclusions drawn. It is to be hoped that before long the Bureau of Labor Statistics will gather information relative to the annual incomes of the workers and also data concerning family incomes. The wage-earner often has a higher real income when working regularly with a relatively low weekly or hourly money wage, than when he works only part time at a comparatively high money wage. It should also be remembered that during periods of prosperity—especially was this true during the years 1916 to 1919—conditions of employment are such that other members of the family can find employment and thereby add to the family income and raise the standard of living. There are no available wage statistics that make possible a study of yearly incomes, and the Bureau of Labor Statistics has not collected figures of wages and employment in a way that makes such a wage computation possible.

Since there are no reliable data available as to the average yearly family income of the wage-earners in general, many people have accepted the relation between the cost of living and union wages as proof that the real wages of labor decreased during the years 1916 to 1919 inclusive. This idea is more readily accepted because it bears out the phenomena so well understood, namely, that wage rates tend to lag behind prices during periods of prosperity. According to the chart, the actual earnings increased more rapidly than cost of living. Is this seeming failure of wages, during the last period of prosperity, to lag behind prices, due to the paucity and consequent unreliability of the wage data? Or is it because the war period was different in this respect from usual periods of prosperity? The latter seems to be the case, if these six industries constitute a representative sample.

In the Cheney Brothers silk-manufacturing establishment of South Manchester, Connecticut, hiring an average of 5,428 employees between 1916 and 1922, the money wages increased faster than the cost of living. Hourly earnings increased from twenty-four cents per hour in 1916 to fifty-nine cents in 1920, and then fell to fifty-three cents in 1922. This is an increase of approximately 142 per cent in 1920 over 1916, which is more than the cost of living increase. Although the wages paid in this one concern can not be taken as representative of the silk industry as a whole, it does throw some further light on the movement of real wages.

Mr. Bing's study of real wages from 1914 to 1919 tends to bear out the same idea.[1] In the ten industries included in his study, four showed substantial increases in real wages. Five showed decreases, while one showed a decrease and then an increase by about the same amount. The two that showed the largest decrease were based upon union wages, and were for industries that had wage contracts which tended to keep the union wages much lower than the actual wages probably were.[2] According to Mr. Bing's wage charts, therefore, a curve of real wages, for those industries for which wage figures were based upon actual hourly compensation, would probably show an increase. This is the same as saying that the curve of money wages, during this period of prosperity, was higher than the curve for cost of living. The relation between the wage curve and the cost-of-living curve in the chart on p. 34, shows the same tendency for real wages to rise, as would probably be shown by a curve of real wages based upon Mr. Bing's figures, although the two sets of figures were computed on different bases and by different methods.

The next question that naturally arises is, why the wage curve should be higher than the curve for the cost of living during this period of rising prices. This can be explained by the abnormal demand for products, due to the warring nations' need for war materials, which led to an unprecedented demand for labor power. In other words, the unusual increase in the demand for labor power, at the same time that the labor force was being rapidly reduced because of the induction of thousands of men into the army, put the laborers in a strong enough bargaining position to enable

[1] See A. M. Bing, *War-Time Strikes and Their Adjustment*, pp. 211-221.

[2] The industries in question were the printers and electrotypers, and the building trades.

them to realize many of their demands for wage increases which otherwise would have been denied. The workers were not long in realizing the importance of being essential to industry, and they took every advantage of their new power to strengthen their position in respect to their employers. It seemed to be common at this time for employers to make special agreements with employees in order to hold them. In fact, employers were often not only willing, but anxious, to pay more than the union rate in order to keep their employees. There are no available figures to show the extent of this practice, but it must have been rather general, since it necessitated, on the part of the government, the fixing of the maximum rates that an employer could pay, as well as minimum rates. This tendency on the part of the employers to pay wages higher than the union rates must have tended to raise the actual wage above the union rates, but we have no way of determining how much.

Th curve of actual wages probably exaggerates the height of wages in 1920, because many of the wage data were collected with the intention of obtaining figures for wages at the highest point in the cycle. In 1921 and 1922 wages probably declined somewhat more rapidly than the curve indicates, because a large per cent of the 1922 figures were gathered for the first part of the year, and therefore, the curve does not show the effect of later wage decreases.

Douglas and Lamberson made a study of real wages from 1912 to 1918,[1] which was a continuation of a study made from 1890 to 1912 by Dr. Rubinow.[2] They found

[1] See Paul H. Douglas and Frances Lamberson, "The Movement of Real Wages, 1890-1918," *American Economic Review*, Sept., 1921, pp. 409-426.

[2] See I. M. Rubinow, "The Recent Trend of Real Wages", *American Economic Review*, Dec., 1914, pp. 798-817.

that real wages decreased between 1912 and 1918. Now let us see to what this difference between their figures and the figures presented here is due. In the first place they made a study of ten industries, three of which were included in this study, and based upon wages taken from the pay-rolls; the other seven industries were based upon union rates.[1] Their figures, therefore, are based primarily on union or minimum rates. We also found that the curve of union rates, as published by the Bureau of Labor Statistics, was below the cost-of-living curve until the first part of 1920, when it rose above the latter. In the second place, fifty per cent of the wage data in this study were taken from the railroad industry, iron and steel industry, and navy yards. These industries were not included in the investigation made by Douglas and Lamberson. The figures in this study are, therefore, based largely upon wages taken from war industries, and consequently are probably higher than figures based upon industries such as baking trades, marble and stone cutters, mill work, etc., not engaged in producing war materials. It seems quite probable, therefore, that if actual wages were available for all the industries included in the study made by Douglas and Lamberson, and if they had used actual rather than union wages, they would have found the average real wage to have been much higher, because in most of the industries where figures of actual wages are available, an increase is shown in real wages between 1917 and 1919 inclusive.

The results of a study made by Professor Ogburn of changes in the wages and cost of living between 1914 and 1918, show the same tendency for actual wages or earnings

[1] The industries included in their study were as follows: baking trades, building trades, foundry and machine work, marble and stone cutters, millwork, book and job printing, newspaper printing, boot and shoe industry, woolen goods, and cotton goods.

to increase faster than the cost of living. According to his figures, earnings of labor increased between 1914 and 1918 in six industries as follows: boot and shoe industry showed an increase of 23.5 per cent, in the cotton-finishing industry, earnings increased 6 per cent, in cotton manufacturing they increased 13 per cent, in hosiery and underwear, the increase was 11 per cent, the silk industry showed an increase of 5 per cent, woolen increased 9 per cent, and earnings in iron and steel increased 45 per cent.[1] He found that the union rates had fallen in sixteen out of nineteen trades, while three out of the nineteen showed slight increases.[2] This unusual increase in the earnings of wage-earners during the war period was due to the restriction of immigration, the drafting of men into military service, government control of wages, increased extension of credit, and the general increased demand for labor power.

It seems, therefore, that while the figures of actual earnings used in this study may exaggerate the height of the wage curve because of the weight given to industries producing war materials, on the other hand, figures based upon union rates are biased in the other direction. But since during this last period of prosperity, a large per cent of American wage-earners were connected with war industries, it seems that if wage figures were computed by taking an average of the actual wages, weighted according to the number of employees in the different industries, the wage curve would be above that for the cost of living until the first part of 1920.

Alvin H. Hansen made a study of the buying power of

[1] See W. F. Ogburn, "Standard of Living as a Basis for Wage Adjustments", *Proceedings of the Academy of Political Science*, 1919, vol. viii, p. 238.

[2] *Ibid*, p. 237.

labor during the war,[1] and found that the laborers' buying power was above " normal " from 1916 to 1920. According to his estimate, the workers' real wage, or buying power, reached its highest point in 1918. His study includes salaried workers whose wages went up slower than the wages of the day workers,[2] and is based upon the total wages paid in industrial establishments rather than upon wage rates, for " pay-rolls, not wage rates, are an index of the buying power of the wage-earning class ". His discussion takes into consideration: (1) changes in wages that the workers received; (2) changes in cost of living; (3) increase in the wage-earning population; (4) the drafting of men and boys into military service; and (5) the flow of agricultural workers into industry.[3] The total amount of wages paid in industry would naturally increase with the growth in population, but an increase in total wages paid, due to an increasing population, would indicate no rise in the workers' real wage, therefore, a correction is made for the increase in population so that the per-capita increase can be calculated.

According to the figures of the United States Census Bureau, Professor Hansen estimates that the industrial wage-earning population increased 21 per cent from 1910 to 1920.[4] He then reduces the wages received by industrial laborers " to a per capita basis by dividing the index numbers of total wages paid (in terms of 1914 prices) by the index numbers of the wage-earning population for the corresponding years ". He also takes account of the number of

[1] See Alvin H. Hansen, "The Buying Power of Labor During the War", *Journal of the American Statistical Association*, March, 1922 pp. 56-66.

[2] *Cf. infra*, p. 31.

[3] Alvin H. Hansen, *loc. cit.*, p. 56.

[4] *Ibid.*, p. 59.

men drawn into military service. In this connection, Professor Hansen estimates that the buying power of labor between 1917 and 1919 was two per cent greater than it would have been had these men not been withdrawn from the laboring population, because the consumption needs of the working population was decreased by this amount, as a result of the induction of an average of 1,451,139 men into military service between 1917 and 1919.[1]

During the war period, there were a large number of agricultural workers who left the farms to go into industry. According to Professor Hansen's estimate, the average addition of agricultural workers for 1917 to the wage-earners gainfully employed in industry must have been less than two per cent.[2] After making allowance for these various factors that influence the buying power of labor, Professor Hansen arrives at the conclusion that the laborers' command over commodities was above normal from 1916 to 1922.[3] His figures for the state of New York and for the United States as a whole are given in the following table.

We are concerned in this work primarily with wages of organized workers, rather than the incomes of the salaried classes, because the latter are not directly connected with the labor movement. Professor Hansen finds that the buying power of labor, including salaried workers, increased during the war period, and naturally we should expect to find that the wages of the day workers increased more during this time than the wages for all classes of industrial workers combined. A comparison of the figures in Table III shows that the difference between the percentage increase

[1] Alvin H. Hansen, *loc. cit.*, p. 61.

[2] *Ibid*, pp. 61-62.

[3] His method of calculating a normal base is discussed on pp. 62-63 of his article.

TABLE IX

PER CAPITA BUYING POWER OF LABOR, 1915-1922

(100 = NORMAL)

Year	New York State	United States
1915	90.0	90.8
1916	107.8	107.9
1917	107.0	109.1
1918	109.6	109.5
1919	101.5	105.9
1920	108.3	108.2
1921	92.7	....
1922	95.3	....

in the cost of living and actual wages is greater than the percentage increase in purchasing power of labor as shown in Table IX. It seems, therefore, that union rates did not adequately measure the wages received by the workers during the war period. In the light of the studies that have been made of real wages during the last period of prosperity, it seems that the workers were in a much stronger economic position, even though prices were rising rapidly, than they were during the following period of depression and falling prices. And according to Professor Hansen's estimate they were receiving higher real wages, as measured by purchasing power, than they were under normal pre-war conditions.

The fact that the curve of general wages is above the cost-of-living curve, does not mean that wages kept up with the increase in prices in all industries, for while wages increased faster than cost of living in some industries, the reverse was true in others. Neither does it mean that in industries where wages kept up with, or even exceeded, the increase in cost of living, the workers were necessarily receiving a living wage, for in many cases, the pre-war wage level was extremely low, and inadequate to keep an average family in "health and reasonable comfort". In such cases, the money wage would have to do more than merely keep up with prices; it would have to increase faster than prices in order to raise the real wage and thereby raise the standard of living.

According to the chart on page 25, the difference between the curve of actual wages and the cost-of-living curve is greater for the years 1920, 1921, and 1922, than for the period of prosperity preceding. This would seem to indicate that the workers had a higher standard of living during the period of depression than during the period of business expansion, which is true for those who retained their positions and worked full time, but since the wage figures do not take into consideration the amount of unemployment, it should not be concluded that wage-earners in general were better off during the years 1920 to 1922.

Hourly earnings give a better index of the trend of general wages during periods of prosperity than during periods of depression; (1) because there is less unemployment and practically no involuntary unemployment on the part of the workers in periods of prosperity except that which is due to illness; and (2) because the effect of time and one half for overtime, bonuses, and special agreements, is reflected in the hourly earnings. But during periods of depression, when thousands of laborers are unemployed, or employed only part time, hourly earnings show what they receive during the hours they actually work, but do not show the influence of unemployment on their incomes. Hourly earnings, therefore, do not constitute an adequate index of wages when there is a large amount of unemployment.

Another point that should be mentioned in this connection, is that fixed salaries rise slower than weekly or daily wages. This was especially true during the last period of business expansion, because women could fill the teaching positions and make efficient clerks, whereas they could not readily enter many other occupations, and the wages of women are usually lower than those of men. Therefore, since the supply of labor was greater for the fixed salary positions, and since a large per cent of this supply was composed of women workers who were willing to work for relatively low wages, and since custom tends to keep such salaries from responding readily to changes in prices, these incomes remained relatively low.

It is estimated that in 1920, there were 3,468,541 males and 2,169,603 females, a total of 5,638,144 persons, classed as "clerks and kindred workers". These figures do not include professional people, public and semi-public officials, and managers for private enterprises. According to the report, the number of "clerks and kindred workers" receiving fixed salaries constitute 13.6 per cent of the total number of persons gainfully employed in the United States. When we consider that 26.8 per cent of the gainfully employed are included among the proprieters, managers, and officials, it means that the total number of wage earners constitute only 59.6 per cent of those gainfully employed.[1] In other words, 22.8 per cent or approximately one fourth of the working people, not including domestic servants, receive fixed salaries. Therefore, since fixed salaries increased less than wages, the one fourth of the workers whose real earnings decreased most during the period of industrial activity are not included in the wage figures. To include them would mean that the curve would be lower than it is.

In the business cycle covering the war period, the response due to the discrepancy between wages in different industries, as well as between wages and prices, was so pronounced on

[1] See A. M. Edwards, "Social-Economic Groups of the United States", *Quarterly Publication of the American Statistical Association*, June, 1917. See also *Monthly Labor Review*, May, 1922, pp. 131-133.

the part of the laboring classes that the government was compelled to create adjustment agencies to handle the situation, in order that production would be unhampered and the war successfully prosecuted.[1] Such a step was not necessary in case of the classes drawing fixed salaries.

The changes in wages in those particular industries mentioned in Table IV and Table VIII show that the percentage increase in those most strongly organized at the beginning of the period of prosperity, was less than in those industries less strongly organized. This was due, in the first place, to the fact that the organized laborers were generally receiving a relatively high wage at first, and then when the principle of adjusting wages to the cost of living was adopted, naturally, the lowest-paid labor got the greatest increase in wage. In the second place, many employers had two and three year wage contracts with their organized employees, which tended to keep wages low. Where such wage contracts existed, they were usually amended, given up, or broken, but often not without much difficulty and delay, during which time prices and the cost of living were rapidly increasing. Therefore, while many labor organizations were endeavoring to get released from their wage contracts, the discrepancy between their union wages and the cost of living was rapidly growing greater and greater.

The effect on wages of strong labor organizations probably was not felt and realized as much during the period of economic activity as during the period of falling prices when pressure was brought to bear by the stronger organizations to keep their wages from falling as rapidly as it was expected they would. This was due to the fact that unorganized as

[1] For a brief statement of the rules and organization of the various adjustment agencies, see *The Report of the Board of Review of Construction to the Assistant Secretary of War*, Aug. 31, 1919, p. 354 *et seq.*

well as organized labor was in a strong bargaining position during the period of prosperity because of the great demand for labor power, and therefore did not feel so great a need for organized protection.

No discussion of wages in its relation to cost of living would be complete without brief mention being made of the influence of certain government agencies, notably the Shipbuilding Labor Adjustment Board.[1] These adjustment boards were compelled to fix maximum as well as minimum rates. The laborers were clamoring for a minimum wage that at least equalled the cost of lving. In some industries employers, in order to keep a steady supply of labor, were bidding against each other and were offering disproportionately high wages; and even certain government departments were competing with each other as well as with outside industries. This led to much unnecessary shifting of labor from one employer to another,[2] which the government endeavored to check by establishing maximum rates that employers could pay.

The National War Labor Board immediately adopted the principle of adjusting wages to the cost of living as measured by the amount necessary to keep a family of five in "health and reasonable comfort". In some cases, wages were raised more than the amount asked by the workers. In one case, for example, wages were increased from twenty-two to forty cents per hour when the men were demanding only thirty cents, because the board found that the cost of living had increased by this amount.[3] In figuring minimum wages overtime was taken into consideration.

[1] See H. B. Drury, "The Labor Policy of the Shipping Board", *Journal of Political Economy*, Jan., 1921, pp. 1-28, for a discussion of the labor policies of the Board.

[2] *Cf. supra*, p. 5.

[3] Decisions of the National War Labor Board, *Docket no. 40*.

While most of the adjustment agencies used similar methods, there were some differences which were reflected in the wages of the industries that came under their jurisdiction.[1] In arriving at a fair wage scale, the Shipbuilding Labor Adjustment Board took into consideration three main factors, namely: (1) the equalization of the wage rates in the shipbuilding centers, so that wages in various ship-yards would not be unreasonably disproportionate; (2) the adjustment of wage rates to the increased cost of living resulting from war conditions; and (3) the establishment of a differential wage in order that shipyard wages might be a little above those in other industries, so as to attract and keep men in the shipbuilding industries. On the East Coast where the workers were not so well organized, wages paid in other industries were considered in arriving at an equitable rate. At first, wages were made uniform in each industry, then later in each district, and finally uniform rates were established for the country as a whole. This policy tended to be followed by most of the other agencies.

The Shipbuilding Labor Adjustment Board said in the Atlantic Coast, Gulf and Great Lake Shipyards decision of October I, 1918,

> We have adopted these uniform national rates because experience has convinced us that by this means only can we put a stop to that shifting of employees from yard to yard and district to district, which continues to be a chief obstacle to efficient ship production. Added arguments for uniform national rates are that citizens working for the Government—and work on ships is now essentially government work—feel that they should all be treated alike; that there are no longer any marked differences in the cost of living between different

[1] For a discussion of the method used by the National Adjustment Commission, see B. M. Squires, "The National Adjustment Commission", *Journal of Political Economy*, July, 1921, pp. 543-570.

sections; and that the United States Employment Service, rather than divergent wage rates with their unsettling tendencies, should be relied upon to effect whatever shifting of wage earners is necessary to the carrying out of the war program.

The Emergency Construction Wage Adjustment Commission accepted the wages and conditions in force on June 1, 1917, as a basic standard for the adjustment of disputes. The wages and conditions were agreed upon by local unions and employers irrespective of whether they were commensurate with the cost of living; consequently rates varied according to the bargaining strength of the two parties at the time the agreement was made. But the effect of this method used by the commission was largely offset by the fact that laborers could shift so easily to other employments and thereby diminish the supply, so that wages in industries that came under the jurisdiction of this commission were more uniform than they otherwise would have been.

Employers often opposed the equalization of wage rates because they could, by rewarding special skill, get greater efficiency. But many of the union leaders favored it, for they saw that collective bargaining became more difficult in direct ratio as individual abilities were recognized. Many labor leaders felt that when men were receiving wages higher than their fellow workmen, they were less interested in organization and collective bargaining.

Never before had the government taken such a leading hand in adjusting wage rates and setting wage standards over the country. The influence of the government in this respect should not be overlooked in studying statistics of wages during this period. Had it not been for the part played by the government in adjusting wages, the real wages in the more strongly organized industries probably would have been much higher than they were, and in many cases wages in unorganized industries would have been much lower; and during the period of prosperity, the labor movement probably would have been more agressive than it was. In some cases, the government threatened to take away the right of exemption from draft if the wage-earners did not return to work, and this, together with the appeal to patriotism, tended to hold the demands of the workers in check.

It is impossible to make an exact quantitative statement of the effect of government regulation on the wage curve, since, as we have seen, wages were affected by a multiplicity of influences; but it is a reasonable inference to draw that there was a closer conformity between wages and the cost of living, due to this regulation, than there otherwise would have been. The part the government played in determining wages is one of the factors that made this period unique and distinctive in our industrial history.

CHAPTER III

Employment and Unemployment

The widespread interest and attention given to the dual problem of employment and unemployment during the extraordinarily severe depression during the latter part of 1920, and 1921 is quite an encouraging sign, for a solution of the problem is dependent to a large extent on the amount of serious thought and attention given to it. In the past, interest in unemployment has usually begun and ended with the depression without any element of permanency, but a more lasting interest in certain problems of employment has sprung up during the last few years. The increased attention given to this problem can be traced to various causes, among the more important of which may be mentioned, first, the element of cost in labor mobility, which has been recognized to such an extent by business men as to cause them to make every effort to stabilize industry. In the second place, enterpreneurs have realized that unemployment does not mean a loss to employees alone, but that it means idle machinery, which constitutes one of the greatest costs in industry. In the third place, some employers fear that unemployment increases radicalism and they hope to keep down the latter by decreasing the former. In the fourth place, the interest in the unemployment problem is due to the realization that unemployment means decreased purchasing power on the part of the workers, which in turn means a limitation of the market for products.[1] This policy of in-

[1] See *The Review of Economic Statistics*, Jan., 1922, p. 12.

creased attention during periods of depression and decreased interest in unemployment during periods of prosperity has been present to a greater or less extent in every business cycle, depending upon its intensity. During periods of depression, unemployment conferences have been called and recommendations have been made for charity relief, part time work, extension of public works, etc., which are not adequate even as a temporary solution. As the depression passes, the problem is forgotten and no effort is made to prepare for handling the situation scientifically when the next depression comes.[1]

Until recently, writers had given very little attention to the relationship between the business cycle and the unemployment problem, and few efforts were made to work out an adequate measure of employment until the present business depression with its attending evils caused the economists to realize the great need for such an index. Measurement of employment aids to an understanding of industrial conditions as well as of the course of the labor market. The index of employment, besides showing changes in employment, measures, first, the purchasing power of the laboring population from current earnings, for even if wage rates remain the same, aggregate earnings change with changes in employment; second, it gives an indirect measure of production except in cases where part-time workers are carried on the pay-roll.

Industrial employment is affected by at least four "distinct movements" or trends, all of which are going on at the same time.[2] In the first place, as population increases

[1] For a discussion of the problem of unemployment see *Report no. 43* of the National Industrial Conference Board, *Bulletin 310* of the Bureau of Labor Statistics, and the *Report of the President's Conference on Unemployment.*

[2] See *Bulletin 310* of the Bureau of Labor Statistics, p. 5.

and industry expands, there is a general increase in the total number of persons employed. In the second place, the volume of employment varies with seasonal variation in industry. In the third place, employment varies with business conditions. And in the fourth place, the labor turnover affects the employment of the individual worker, for he is usually unemployed, for a few days at least, before he finds another position. This last phenomenon is measured by statistics dealing with labor turnover and is not included in the unemployment statistics.

Statistics of employment or unemployment are significant only in so far as they reflect or measure continuous employment or unemployment.

The statement that at a certain time in a given city 200,000 workers are unemployed, or that 16.2 per cent of the wage earners of New York were out of work on February 1, 1915, is of little significance for our purposes. It does not tell us how long they were out of work; it marks only the height of the crest of one wave, not the wave length.[1]

In the last few years, several indices of employment have been computed with special reference to the business cycle.

The four most important of these indices of the volume of employments are those of the Bureau of Labor Statistics, New York State, Wisconsin, and Massachusetts. Ethelbert Stewart, United States Commissioner of Labor, has made a comparison of these four indices of employment.[2]

The Bureau of Labor Statistics' index overweights the

[1] See *Bulletin 310* of the Bureau of Labor Statistics, p. 7.

[2] See *Monthly Labor Review*, March, 1922, pp. 1-7. See also, W. A. Berridge, "Employment and the Business Cycle", *Review of Economic Statistics*, January, 1922. pp. 15-16, and by the same author, "Cycles of Employment and Unemployment in the United States, 1914-1921", *Journal of the American Statistical Association*, March, 1922, pp. 42-55, and June, 1922, pp. 227-240.

textile industry, and in this respect, cotton introduces, to a considerable extent, the effect of crop variation, which is largely independent of the business cycle.[1] According to the study made by Berridge, the Bureau of Labor Statistics' index combined with that of New York State and corrected for seasonal variation, etc., constitutes the best current index of employment. This combination seems to come nearer filling the requirements of a good current index because (a) " its components " are reported in a comparable form for a period sufficiently long to serve as a basis for comparison and appraisal; (b) because it is industrially and geographically representative; and (c) because the figures are reported in monthly form with reasonable accuracy and promptness.[2] The figures of the Bureau of Labor Statistics are based upon the returns of 750 establishments in thirteen leading industries located in thirty-one states.[3] Some establishments failed to report at times, with the result that the number of establishments varies from month to month.

The Bureau of Labor Statistics' index numbers of employment fall short of showing the actual " increase in the number of persons employed in the manufacturing industry in the United States as a whole between 1914 and 1918, as according to the census the increase was 29.3 per cent." [4]

[1] See W. A. Berridge, " Cycles of Employment and Unemployment in the United States, 1914-1921," *Journal of the American Statistical Association*, March, 1922, pp. 46 and 47.

[2] *Ibid*, pp. 49-51.

[3] The industries included were as follows: boots and shoes, cotton manufacturing, hosiery and underwear, woolen, silk, men's ready-made clothing, iron and steel, car-building and repairing, cigar manufacturing, automobile manufacturing, leather manufacturing, paper making, and cotton finishing. The industries included in the New York index were as follows: metals and machinery; textiles; clothing; furs, leather, and rubber goods; food, beverages, and tobacco; printing and paper goods; paper; chemicals, oils, paints, etc.; wood manufacturing; stone, clay, and glass products; water, light and power.

[4] See *Monthly Labor Review*, March, 1922, p. 4.

But the combined index of New York and of the Bureau of Labor Statistics tends to correct many of the shortcomings of either one of the indices used separately.

It is estimated by the United States Employment Service that for American industry as a whole, the number of people employed in January, 1921, was over three million less than in 1920. In 1424 concerns employing 500 or more persons in 65 of the leading industrial centers, the employment was three per cent less in April, 1921, than in January, 1921. In August, 1921, employment had gone up 1.08 per cent over July. Employment decreased between 20 and 25 per cent between July, 1920, and August, 1921.[1] This estimate was made by taking the difference in the number on the payrolls at the peak of employment in 1920 and July, 1921.

During 1921 and 1922, the majority of unemployment was involuntary on the part of the workers, and due to conditions that they could not prevent. According to Babson, the index number of the persons employed in 1921 remained below the June, 1914, index until the very last of the year, and during 1922, it was practically the same as the 1914 index of employment until the last of the year when it rose a little above the 1914 figure.[2] The following table gives the figures of employment from 1915 to 1922:

[1] See the *United States Industrial Employment Survey Bulletin, no. 1* and 7, and the last *Report of the President's Conference on Unemployment*, September 26, 1921, pp. 52-56, *passim*, and E. S. Bradford, "Methods Used in Measuring Employment", *Journal of the American Statistical Association*, December, 1921, pp. 983-984.

[2] See *Babson's Statistical Tables and Charts*.

TABLE X

GENERAL INDICES OF EMPLOYMENT IN THE UNITED STATES,[1]
1915-1922

(Unit: one-tenth of one standard deviation)

Year	January	February	March	April	May	June	July	August	September	October	November	December
1915	—16	—16	—16	—15	—13	—11	—11	—10	— 7	— 5	— 4	— 3
1916	— 3	— 2	— 1	+ 1	+ 0	+ 2	+ 2	+ 4	+ 5	+ 6	+ 7	+ 6
1917	+ 8	+ 7	+ 7	+ 5	+ 6	+ 6	+ 7	+ 6	+ 5	+ 7	+ 7	+ 8
1918	+ 7	+ 6	+ 7	+ 6	+ 6	+ 7	+10	+ 9	+ 8	+ 4	+ 5	+ 4
1919	+ 0	— 4	— 5	— 4	— 4	— 1	+ 2	+ 4	+ 3	+ 1	+ 2	+ 5
1920	+ 7	+ 6	+ 7	+ 8	+ 7	+ 7	+ 4	+ 5	+ 1	— 1	— 9	—16
1921	—22	—20	—20	—20	—20	—19	—19	—18	—18	—16	—17	—17
1922	—18	—17	—19	—20	—19	—16	—16	—14	—13	— 9	— 9	— 7

The chart presents graphically the relation between business conditions and employment. It shows that there is a very close relationship between the volume of employment and the curve of business conditions. This is to be expected because of the methods used in computing the indices of business conditions and employment.[2] The curve of business conditions is based upon physical production, which in turn is dependent, to a large extent, upon the volume of employment. This curve rises more rapidly during the latter part of 1915 than the employment curve, which is probably due, in part, to the fact that many men had been taken on as part-time workers in an effort to alleviate the unemployment of 1914 and the first of 1915. These men were carried on the pay-roll and therefore, were listed

[1] *Cf. supra*, p. 42.

[2] See W. A. Berridge, "Cycles of Employment and Unemployment in the United States, 1903-1914", *Journal of the American Statistical Association*, June, 1922, p. 240.

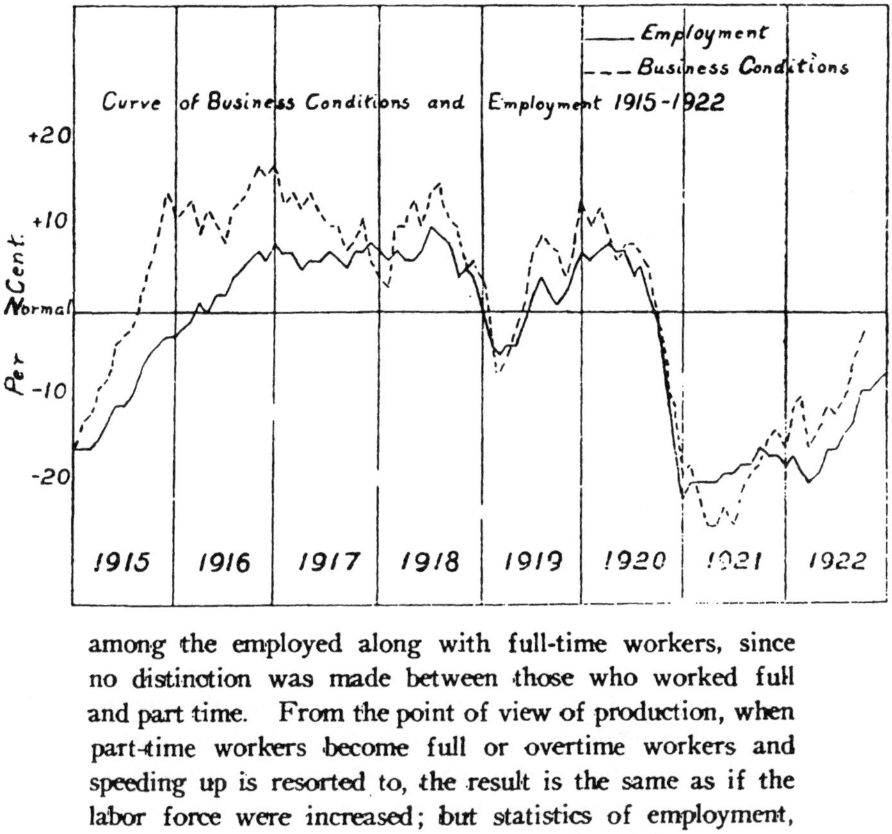

among the employed along with full-time workers, since no distinction was made between those who worked full and part time. From the point of view of production, when part-time workers become full or overtime workers and speeding up is resorted to, the result is the same as if the labor force were increased; but statistics of employment, gathered from the pay-rolls, are not affected in any way by such changes. The volume of physical production, therefore, could be increased considerably by speeding up and working overtime, without increasing the number of employees on the payroll. But speeding up and overtime work can hardly account for the great difference between the curves during the latter part of 1915. The difference is probably due more to the fact that the business curve is based upon physical production, and many of the items included in the index—for example, pig-iron production—show great fluctuations during the war period. It may be that these unusual fluctuations are largely responsible for the character of the business curve during this period. The Harvard Committee found that some of the items which they had included in the business group had lost their value as an index of business conditions after the outbreak of the war in 1914. This was explained on the grounds that abnormal economic conditions, government control of industry, and changes in economic organization caused them to fluctuate to a greater extent, and more erratically than they did under normal conditions. According to this, then, the curve should indicate that business conditions fluctuated more widely than employment. The curves show this to be the case, and therefore, tend to bear out the opinion that the business curve is influenced considerably by items that fluctuate violently.

The difference between the two curves in 1915 may also be due in large part to the influence of price changes. During this time the business index included items that were affected by price, and these items, therefore, would tend to influence the business index in accordance with price changes.

The curve of business conditions falls below the employment curve in the latter part of 1917, in the latter part of 1918, and the first part of 1919, and again in the middle of 1921. This is probably due to the fact that entrepreneurs are inclined to carry men on the pay-roll for a time after prosperity ceases, until they are convinced that a depression has started. This "carry-over" of employees means that employment decreases less during the beginning of a depression, than prices, profits, production, etc.

The increase in employment during 1915 and 1916 was due to the increased demand of the European nations for American products, when their own resources were being depleted so rapidly. This increased demand for products naturally meant a larger demand for labor power, especially after our entrance into the war. By the middle of 1917, all available men had been taken into industry and still the supply of labor was not equal to the demand; but the employment curve could not go higher, except through the women going into industry. The drop in the employment curve in the middle of 1917 was due largely to the influence of the draft which took men from industry for military service. But this was soon overcome by women flocking into industry to take the places of the men, and the curve of employment rose again and continued to waver slightly until September and October of 1918 when there was a decided drop. This was due, in large part, to the influenza epidemic which caused much unemployment, as well as to the general feeling that the war would soon end with an allied victory. It was generally believed that there would be an automatic deflation of prices with the return of the soldiers to industry, the conversion of war industries to peace-time production, and the " general let-down from maximum war production ". Indices of business conditions seemed to indicate that a period of reaction and deflation was approaching. The production of coal, iron, coke, and crude steel fell off very much, which seemed to bear out the general belief of coming deflation. The index number of employment declined as a result of these conditions.[1]

The curve then shows the results of the Armistice and the consequent slight depression in the first part of 1919 with the recovery by the middle or latter part of the year. The sudden and precipitate fall during the latter part of 1920 reflects rather accurately the intensity of the depression. The following table shows the great increase in unemployment in particular industries:

[1] See *Report no. 408* of the Joint Commission of Agricultural Inquiry, Oct., 1921, p. 41.

TABLE XI

PER CENT OF DECREASE IN EMPLOYMENT IN SPECIFIED INDUSTRIES BETWEEN JANUARY 1920 AND JANUARY 1921 [1]

Industry	Per Cent Decrease
Mechanical Industries [2]	36.9
Metal products, machinery, electrical and foundry products	30.5
Building trades	52.4
Packing and food products	19.0
Textile products, clothing, hosiery and underwear	35.5
Leather, boots and shoes	34.9
Automobiles and accessories	69.2
Lumber, furniture and wood products	32.3
Clay, glass, cement and stone products.	19.3
Average	36.6

The figures in this table show the same tendency regarding unemployment as is shown by the unemployment curve, namely, that there was an unprecedented increase in unemployment, or, which is the same thing, decrease in employment between January, 1920, and January, 1921. During 1921, the employment curve wavers, following in general, the curve of business conditions.

While it is impossible to measure the effect of strikes on employment or unemployment, an explanation of the fluctuations in the employment curve would be incomplete without calling attention to the influence of strikes and lockouts. The Bureau of Labor Statistics has no authority to require reports relative to strikes and lockouts, but it has kept a record of all strikes that have come to its attention. The information was obtained by agents of the Bureau, reports

[1] See *American Labor Legislation Review*, Sept., 1921, pp. 191-217.

[2] Railroads and Mining groups are not included.

of state labor boards, lists of strikes issued by various trades and labor organizations, clippings from newspapers. labor periodicals, etc.[1] Many of the smaller and less important fluctuations in the curve are probably due to strikes that happened to be taking place in the industries investigated at the time of the investigation. Since the figures for employment were taken from the pay-rolls they are directly influenced by the duration of the strikes as well as the number of employees out on strikes. The following table shows the number of employees on strike between 1916 and 1921:

TABLE XII

NUMBER OF PERSONS INVOLVED IN STRIKES AND LOCKOUTS, 1916 TO 1921 [2]

Year	Strikes	Lockouts	Total
1916	1,546,735	53,182	1,599,917
1917	1,208,121	19,133	1,227,254
1918	1,196,928	43,061	1,239,989
1919	3,992,585	162,148	4,154,733
1920	1,417,456	17,736	1,435,192
1921	998,805	86,848	1,085,653
Total	10,370,630	382,108	10,742,738

Table XII shows the large increase in the number of persons on strike in 1919. While there were not as many

[1] The number of strikes and lockouts beginning in each year from 1916 to 1921 inclusive were as follows: 3,789 in 1916; 4,450 in 1917; 3,353 in 1918; 3,577 in 1919; 3,254 in 1920; and 2,267 in 1921. More strikes and lockouts were begun in May of each year, than in any other month. This was due to the fact that many union contracts ended the last of April, and disagreements in drawing up new contracts led to an inincreased number of labor disputes.

[2] See *Monthly Labor Review*, May, 1922, p. 186. Reliable information concerning strikes and lockouts for 1915 is not available. Data for 1922 are not available except for a few months.

strikes in 1919 as there were in 1917, there were a larger number of persons involved and the strikes were of longer duration. The influence of strikes on unemployment can be seen better by comparing the number of persons out on strike, with the duration of the trikes as given in Table XIII. It is impossible to estimate the influence of strikes on employment by merely giving the number of people involved without considering the duration of the strike. The amount of employment might be decreased much more by a few employees out for a long time than by a large number out for only a few days.

TABLE XIII

DURATION OF STRIKES AND LOCKOUTS[1]

Time	1916 Per cent of total	1917 Per cent of total	1918 Per cent of total	1919 Per cent of total	1920 Per cent of total	1921 Per cent of total
2 days or less	17.2	28.7	24.0	9.4	11.9	8.3
3 to 6 days	24.3	18.9	21.8	14.2	14.3	12.7
7 to 14 days	24.0	21.4	23.0	18.8	22.1	16.7
15 to 31 days	18.1	14.6	17.2	21.7	19.5	16.6
32 to 91 days	10.3	11.6	10.5	26.2	20.7	27.1
92 to 200 days	4.6	3.9	1.8	8.3	9.3	14.6
Over 200 days	1.0	.7	1.2	1.2	2.3	3.9

The percentage of the total number of strikes and lockouts reported between 1916 and 1921 without information as to duration is as follows: 13.9 per cent in 1916, 31.6 per cent in 1917, 22.9 per cent in 1918, 14.8 per cent in 1919, 26.2 per cent in 1920, and 19.5 per cent in 1921.

One of the most significant features of the above table is the relatively large number of strikes that lasted for a

[1]Compiled from the *Monthly Labor Review*, May, 1922, p. 189. Includes only those strikes and lockouts for which information was given as to duration.

very short period of time in 1917 and 1918. For example, 47.6 and 45.8 per cent of the strikes for 1917 and 1918 respectively lasted for a period of six days or less. On the other hand, the corresponding percentages for 1919, 1920, and 1921 were 23.6, 26.2, and 21.0 respectively.

The above two tables, taken together, indicate that employment statistics were influenced much more by the strikes in 1919 and 1920 than by the strikes in any of the other years, since there were more laborers out on strike during these years, and since the strikes were of longer duration.

The large number of strikes during 1917 and 1918 that lasted only a few days seems to indicate that the employers were meeting many of the workers' demands, and also indicates the restlessness and dissatisfaction of laborers in general.

The following table is interesting because it shows the total number of strikes and lockouts for each year as well as the principal causes of strikes:

TABLE XIV

THE PRINCIPAL CAUSES OF STRIKES AND LOCKOUTS BEGINNING IN 1916, 1917, 1918, 1919, 1920, and 1921 [1]

Causes	1916	1917	1918	1919	1920	1921
Increase of wages. .	1301	1571	1397	1074	1327	118
Decrease of wages. .	35	36	36	86	141	866
Acts of employers. .	42	357	312	286	347	175
Acts of employees. .	495	1253	837	1598	877	715
Miscellaneous . . .	285	421	310	285	260	233
Not reported . . .	631	812	461	248	302	160
Total	2789	4450	3353	3577	3254	2267

[1] Compiled from the *Monthly Labor Review*, June, 1920, p. 204, and May, 1922, p. 185.

According to this table, the largest number of strikes occurred in 1917. This is not surprising since cost of living was advancing much more rapidly than union wages at this time, and the government agencies had not had time to work out standards and methods for readily adjusting disputes.

One of the most interesting points to notice in the above table is the decrease in strikes in 1921 caused by demands for higher wages. In 1917 there were 1571 strikes for increased pay as compared to 118 in 1921. On the other hand, there was an increase in number of strikes, caused by decreased wages, from 36 in 1917 and 1918 to 866 in 1921. This seems to show fairly conclusively that the character of the strikes was changing from the offensive to the defensive.

It might be well to mention at this point the influence of the government on strikes. Although the government agencies for adjusting disputes, declared that workers in war industries should not go on strike, and the various governmental departments and commissions cooperated in an effort to keep down strikes, it can be seen from Table XIV, that their attempts were not successful. The National War Labor Board, for example, declared that no strike should be called when a decision was pending, and that both sides should abide by the awards of the Board. Although the Board had no compulsory powers, its decisions were often enforced by extra-legal methods. For instance, the President, who had gained extreme powers during this abnormal period, sometimes brought pressure to bear in such a way as practically to give compulsory powers to the Board. This is illustrated by the case of the striking machinists of Bridgeport, Connecticut. The machinists refused to accept the award of the National War Labor Board. When President Wilson heard of their refusal to abide by the decision of the Board, he wrote them a letter ordering them to return to work. In speaking of their refusal to accept the Board's award, he said:

If such disregard of the solemn adjudication of a tribunal to which both parties submitted their claims be temporized with, agreements become mere scraps of paper. If errors creep into awards, the proper remedy is submission to the award with an application for rehearing to the tribunal. But to strike against the award is disloyalty and dishonor. . . .

Therefore, I desire that you return to work and abide by the award. If you refuse, each of you will be barred from employment in any war industry in the community in which the strike occurred for a period of one year. During that time the United States Employment Service will decline to obtain employment for you in any war industry elsewhere in the United States, as well as under the War and Navy Departments, the Shipping Boards, the Railroad Administration, and other government agencies, and the draft board will be instructed to reject any claim of exemption based on your alleged usefulness in war production.

This threat practically amounted to a governmental blacklist and a withdrawal of draft exemption on industrial grounds, and shows to what extreme lengths the government was ready to go in order to insure continuous production.

Mr. Bing tells how the "draft boards were used in many places for the purpose of intimidation and to break up strikes." The draft boards and committees that had jurisdiction over questions of exemption were composed largely of lawyers and business men who were often not in sympathy with labor.

The rules provided that if a worker had been granted exemption from the draft on the ground of his industrial need to the community and thereafter left his job, it was the duty of the employer to notify the draft board of this fact. . . . The trouble was that if there was talk of a strike, the employer would threaten the worker with the revocation of draft exemption, and immediately upon the occurrence of a strike would notify the draft board that the men had left his employment. Thereupon, the board would quickly put him back in class 1-A and the man would in a few days be taken to camp. In most cases the draft board knew perfectly well that the man had not permanently left his employment, but that he was taking part in a strike.[1]

In this way, many skilled men who were needed in industry were inducted into military service. While such drastic methods of intimidation kept some men from going on strikes, it probably caused more harm and unemployment by increasing dissatisfaction and mobility, than it did good in reducing the number of strikes and unemployment.

[1] See A. M. Bing, War-Time Strikes and Their Adjustment, pp. 233-234.

CHAPTER IV

Labor Mobility and Absenteeism

A study of labor instability shows that it is generally the result of (1) fluctuations in industrial activity, including seasonal and cyclical changes, which cause the amount of employment available for workers to fluctuate, (2) dissatisfaction of the workers with their jobs, and (3) dissatisfaction of employers with their employees. It is the first of these causes that is of interest to us in following the influence of industrial activity upon labor mobility.[1]

Labor mobility, as the term is used here, includes both the accessions to and separations from industry on the part of the workers. The quitting rate, lay-off rate, and discharge rate taken together constitute the separation rate. The flux rate or labor flux includes both the separation and accession rates. The aggregate number of hours actually worked by all of the employees is taken as the standard work force with which the number of labor changes is compared. This standard is used because it " is a genuine standard base, in as much as it actually represents the volume of employment or the amount of industrial exposure. This base at once eliminates all inflation due to ' dead ' and ' broken-time ' names on pay-roll, putting establishments with varying amounts of employment on a par and thus making possible

[1] See S. H. Slichter, *The Turnover of Factory Labor,* (New York, 1919), Ch. v, for a discussion of causes of labor turnover, and Paul F. Brissenden and Emil Frankel, *Labor Turnover in Industry,* (New York, 1922), *passim.*

the strictest comparability ".[1] The flux rate per 10,000 labor hours is equal to the

$$\frac{\text{accessions} + \text{separations}}{\text{number of labor hours worked}} \times 10{,}000;$$ the accession rate equals the $$\frac{\text{accessions}}{\text{number of labor hours}} \times 10{,}000;$$ the separation rate equals the $$\frac{\text{separations}}{\text{number of labor hours}} \times 10{,}000.$$[2] A good illustration of this method of figuring labor turnover is given by the authors.

A separation rate of 1.0 per full-year (3,000 hour) worker, as the Bureau of Labor Statistics has lately computed mobility rates, or a separation rate (called according to the Rochester method "percentage of turnover") of 100 per hundred on the work force, as the Bureau formerly figured "turnover", are both equivalent to a separation rate of 3.3 per unit of 10,000 labor hours. . . .[3]

The general extent of mobility is figured by comparing the accessions and separations in a given period with the number of labor hours put in by the work force during that period. A rate of 3.3 is equal to a complete turnover of work force, because a full year for one laborer constitutes approximately 3,000 labor hours. When there is one change for each 3,000 labor hours it means a complete

[1] See Paul F. Brissenden and Emil Frankel, "The Mobility of Industrial Labor", *Political Science Quarterly*, Dec., 1920, p. 571.

[2] *Ibid*, Dec., 1920, pp. 566-600. See also Paul F. Brissenden, "The Measurement of Labor Mobility", Journal of Political Economy, June, 1920, pp. 441-476. For a comparison of various methods of figuring labor turnover, see *Monthly Labor Review*, June, 1918, pp. 172-173, and June, 1920, p. 39. See also *American Economic Review*, June, 1919, pp. 402-405, December, 1919, pp. 903-905, and March, 1920, pp. 106-108.

[3] See Paul F. Brissenden and Emil Frankel, "Mobility of Labor in American Industry," *Monthly Labor Review*, June, 1920, p. 39.

labor turnover; consequently with 10,000 labor hours, a rate of 3.3 means a complete turnover of the work force. Some writers object to using replacements as the numerator, in computing labor turnover; but there is little objection to using the average number on the pay-roll as a denominator, for the use of average attendance as the denominator confuses absenteeism and turnover.[1] They hold that separations rather than replacements should be used. There is very little difference between the two methods when the working force is increasing, since more are being hired than are leaving, so that the separation rate is equal to the replacement rate. The two methods differ very much, however, when the work force is decreasing, i. e., when more men are leaving than are being hired. Separations do not equal replacements in this case.

Those who favor using separations as a measure of labor turnover do so because they are interested primarily in the degree to which employment is continuous. " The use of this method, however, does not distinguish between (1) the number of men that must be hired to maintain a working force at a given level and (2) a decrease in that level ". Separations include both of these factors, but the causes and cost of the two are quite different. Separations may be due to a reduction of working force, and such separations are not expensive to the entrepreneurs, while replacements are expensive, due to the cost incurred in training new men. It seems, therefore, that the replacements and separations should be distinguished. It matters very little what names are applied to these phenomena, as long as it is made clear just what is meant in each case. If one wishes to speak of the separations as " labor turnover ", then one should use some other term to designate replacements *per se*. We are

[1] See *American Economic Review*, March, 1920, p. 106-108.

not particularly interested here in the rate at which men are leaving industry, but rather with the rate at which those who leave are replaced. The separations due to a reduction of the working force, are not replaced and are, therefore, taken care of by the unemployment figures. Other separations are replaced, and included in the "labor turnover" as the term is used in these pages.

The following table shows the extent of labor turnover between 1916 and 1919. The figures were compiled from data gathered by the Bureau of Labor Statistics:

TABLE XV

LABOR MOBILITY RATE PER 10,000 LABOR HOURS AND PER CENT OF UNNECESSARY CHANGES [1]

Year	Labor Changes			
	Accessions	Separations	Total flux	Per cent of actual changes unnecessary
1915	2.6	2.1	4.7	—
1916	4.6	3.6	8.2	67
1917	4.6	4.3	8 9	78
1917-18	6.9	6.7	13.6	86
1918	5 8	5.0	10.8	78
1919	3.0	2.8	5.8	68

These figures were gathered by the Bureau of Labor Statistics through field investigations supplemented by correspondence. The survey covered approximately 260 establishments employing over 500,000 workers in 17 states. In any given year the rate of turnover is represented by either the accession or separation rate, depending on which is the smaller. During the period, 1917-18,

[1] See Paul F. Brissenden and Emil Frankel, "Mobility of Labor in American Industry," *Monthly Labor Review*, June, 1920, p. 41.

there were more than four labor changes for each full-year worker in the aggregate work force. This is as if during these twelve months all the employees had left their jobs, an entirely new set had come in to fill their places, and afterward all the employees in this second set had left their jobs and had in turn been fully replaced by a third set of workers.[1]

The effect of industrial conditions on the mobility rate is shown by the marked tendency of labor turnover to increase during the period of industrial activity. Table XV shows that the rates were highest during the period, 1917-18, when the demand for war materials and necessities caused a great increase in the demand for production. It was also at this time that many men were being drafted into the army and their places were being filled by women, and men exempt from the draft. These figures were taken from industries that kept records of their labor mobility, which would seem to indicate that they gave more attention to the problem than most industries do. If it were possible to get figures for the majority of the leading industries in the country, the rate of turnover would without doubt be much higher than the above figures indicate. Most of American industries give very little attention to their labor mobility and its control.

A study of mobility rates by particular industries shows that those industries most closely connected with producing war necessities had the highest mobility rates. Examples of such industries are automobile, chemical, leather and rubber goods, machine manufacturing, etc.

It is estimated that from 25 to 35 per cent of the work force must be replaced each year due to the necessary separations. But even if we allow for this necessary replacement and also allow for the necessary increase in the labor force

[1] Brissenden and Frankel, *op. cit.*, p. 42.

to take care of the expansion in industry during 1917-18 there still remain many changes in the labor force that were not necessary. This is shown by the figures of unnecessary labor changes in the table above.

During the year 1917-18, the rate of mobility for the unskilled was over three times that for the skilled. The following table gives the mobility rates for skilled and unskilled in 1917-18:

TABLE XVI

RATE OF MOBILITY PER 10,000 LABOR HOURS IN 1917-18[1]

	Accessions	Separations	Flux
Skilled	4.5	5.1	9.6
Unskilled	14.9	14.5	29.4
Total	6.7	7.1	13.8[2]

This high rate of labor mobility and turnover is significant because of the costs to both the employers and the employees. But laborers more often gain than lose by a change during periods of prosperity, while the reverse is true during periods of depression. During periods of industrial activity, a large percent of turnover is voluntary on the part of the workers. They change usually to take jobs that pay more, but their gains in this respect are often more than offset by enforced separations and changes during periods of depres-

[1] See *Monthly Labor Review*, June, 1920, p. 46.

[2] The difference between the accession, separation, and flux rates for 1917-1918 given in Table XV and in this table is probably due to some workers who were unclassified according to skill, and therefore were not included in this table, but were included in computing the labor mobility rates as given in Table XV.

sion. Especially was this true in the last business depression as is evidenced by the unprecedented unemployment of the latter part of 1920, and 1921. In general, labor mobility is more costly to employers than it appears to be at first sight. It is estimated that the cost of breaking in a new man varies from fifty to three hundred dollars, and yet the cost of labor turnover and mobility has been quite generally ignored by employers in the past. But as production has become more standardized and entrepreneurs operate on a smaller per-unit profit, the problem of costs due to labor turnover has begun to attract widespread attention.[1]

The figures of labor mobility and turnover do not include the transfer of men from one department to another, which, according to Mr. Slichter, amounts to the same thing as firing and then rehiring by another department. He considers this as one of the more important factors in labor turnover.[2]

The cost of labor turnover during the recent period of business expansion becomes more significant if we consider the cost incident to training new men, in connection with the figures for unnecessary labor changes. We have seen that in a work force of over 500,000 persons, there were more than four labor changes for each full-year worker

[1] For a discussion of the cost of labor turnover see "Slichter, *op. cit. passim*", and John R. Commons, *Trade Unionism and Labor Problems*, Second Series (New York, 1921), p. 158, G. S. Watkins, *An Introduction to the Study of Labor Problems* (New York, 1922), p. 260, and *Monthly Labor Review*, June, 1918, pp. 172-173.

[2] It hardly seems accurate to include such changes in labor turnover. There is no unemployment caused by such changes, and it means a saving rather than a loss to the employer, when the worker is put in the place where he is best suited. Again, labor turnover proper means a loss to the employer, due to idle machinery, while changes within the industry do not cause such a loss. Since, therefore, the transfer of men from one department to another, affects unemployment and costs so much less than does labor turnover, it seems that the two should not be classed together.

during 1917-1918.[1] This is the same as if three different men had worked at each job during the year, which means that, roughtly, one and one third out of every two of the changes could have been avoided, because they were due to causes and conditions that should be eliminated. If it costs on an average between fifty and three hundred dollars to train new men, it can be seen what it must have cost to train an average of one and one third more men than were necessary, since, according to the figures, approximately two thirds of the labor changes were unnecessary. If we take the minimum average cost of fifty dollars per man, it means that the cost due to unnecessary labor turnover in the establishments investigated was increased on the average by sixty-five dollars for every job. It is little wonder then that at least some employers are beginning to give the problem serious attention. Of course we must remember that not all new men employed have to be trained. A large percent of the labor changes are often among men who are trained in their respective fields and can go to a new plant and take up the work without any additional cost to the employer. In such cases, the cost to the employer is incurred because of the idle machinery until the vacancies are filled. But during the war, an unusually large percent of the new men employed in the various plants had to be trained for the work, which increased the costs to the employers.

There are probably two reasons why this problem is given more consideration now than in the past. In the first place, entrepreneurs in general are operating on a smaller margin of profit per unit now than ever before. This is due to more government regulation of business, to better standardized business methods, to reduced costs of production, and finally, to a realization on the part of employers that often a greater profit can be made by selling larger amounts at a smaller

[1] See Table xv and the discussion following.

profit per unit, than smaller amounts at a larger profit. Since they are operating on a smaller per-unit profit, it causes them to give more attention to their costs. In the second place, employers are less likely to be careful about their costs in time of business expansion than they are in times of depression. But in times of depression, there is very little replacement of laborers, or labor turnover as we have defined it. Therefore, at times when employers are forced to reduce their costs, there is very little labor turnover, and when there is a large percent of turnover, employers have less inducement to reduce costs.

In discussing the effect of labor mobility and turnover upon the American labor movement, it is necessary to say something concerning voluntary turnover, which has a peculiar significance in its effect upon employment, and also upon the attitude of the workers in general. In a study of voluntary labor turnover made by E. J. Benge,[1] it was found that those employees with a good education and salary had a relatively low rate of turnover. The study included 4,379 employees, of which 3,984 were white, 337 colored, and 58 unknown. The turnover among the Negroes was higher than among the whites. According to years of education, those with eight years had the highest rate of turnover, and it decreased very rapidly with education above eight years. Those with high wages also had a relatively low turnover rate as is shown by Table XVII. According to the table, laborers who were receiving more than sixty cents per hour, had a much lower voluntary turnover rate than those who were receiving less. If we consider what this means in regard to the labor movement, we must come to the conclusion that dissatisfaction among poorly paid workers is much

[1] E. J. Benge, "How to Analyze the Working Force", *Management Engineering*, Feb., 1922, pp. 79-84. Mr. Benge is Director of Office Employment for the Atlantic Refining Company.

greater than among the higher paid laborers. In other words, dissatisfaction among the laboring classes tends to vary inversely with their wages. We can, therefore, see

TABLE XVII

ANALYSIS OF VOLUNTARY TURNOVER ACCORDING TO WAGES PER HOUR[1]

(Jan. to May 1921 inclusive)

Wages Cts. Per Hr.	Resigned		On Roll		Turnover
	Number	Per cent	Number	Per cent	Per cent
20 to 29	6	0.9	39	.9	15.3
30 to 39	28	4.3	212	4.8	13.2
40 to 49	401	61.9	2173	49.6	18.4
50 to 59	138	21.3	888	20.3	15.6
60 to 69	35	5.4	540	12.3	6.5
70 to 79	31	4.8	351	8.0	8.8
80 to 89	. .	. .	9	0.2	
90 to 99	.	. .	3	0.1	
Piece work	9	1.4	64	1.5	13.1
Unknown	.	. .	100	2.3	
Total	648	100	4379	100	14.8

that labor troubles will of necessity become worse during periods when cost of living is rising faster than wages, for the real wages are falling at such times. In periods of falling prices when employers attempt to reduce wages, the workers immediately feel that a reduction in their money wage means a still greater reduction in purchasing power, since they are inclined to think of their income in terms of dollars and cents. In other words, a high rate of voluntary turnover usually means a high degree of dissatisfaction, which in turn causes an increased number of strikes and lockouts with their attending unemployment. Such conditions

[1] The figures in the table are not applicable to industry in general, except in so far as this one plant was representative.

tend to increase the misunderstanding and antagonism between employer and employees. When we consider that the figures of voluntary turnover were taken from the period between January and May, 1921, they have still greater significance. This was a period of business depression and unemployment. Laborers were not ready to give up their places unless they had very goood reasons for doing so. Therefore, the large amount of voluntary turnover at this time tends to emphasize still more the extent of the dissatisfaction that must have prevailed among the workers.

In periods of prosperity when it is hard to keep a steady, well-trained, and efficient labor force, the employers' position is relatively weakened and that of the workers' strengthened. Thus the labor movement gained in strength decidedly during the period of prosperity when employers were willing to concede and grant many of the demands of labor in an effort to keep a steady labor force, because a cessation of work at this time meant a large loss in profits to the employing class.

Reliable statistics relating to labor turnover from 1919 to date are not available, but the figures of unemployment during the depression show that the separation rate increased very much while practically no new men were added until the latter part of 1921 when the trough of the depression was passed. This means that the replacement rate of labor turnover was practically negligible during this period. Wage-earners, in general, were trying to hold their jobs and the gains that they had made during the period of prosperity. This is evidenced by the character of the strikes which took place during this time. Most of the strikes and dissatisfaction on the part of workers were due to wage cuts rather than refusal of employers to raise wages. In other words, the labor movement was now characterized by the employers taking the offensive and the employees the defensive.

Closely connected with labor mobility is the problem of labor absenteeism. Some writers make little or no distinction between the two, but if we define labor absenteeism as either the voluntary or involuntary absence of employees from work while their names are carried on the pay-roll, it is obvious that the two terms are not synonymous and, therefore should not be treated as if they were. J. D. Hackett defines absenteeism as a "temporary cessation of work for not less than one whole working day on the initiative of the worker when his presence in the plant is expected by the employer".[1] It is true that often employees are carried on the pay-roll and treated as absentees when they have permanently severed their connection with the plant, but failure on the part of the employers to keep up with their employees is not sufficient justification for failing to distinguish between the two terms.

Labor absenteeism is directly responsible for a large per cent of the labor turnover, because, as has been said, "the absent employee of to-day is quite likely to become a factor in the labor mobility of to-morrow". Especially is this true during periods of prosperity, for, if jobs are plentiful, the more the wage-earner stays away from his work, the more likelihood there is that he will give up his place and seek new employment. While there are few available figures on which an estimate can be based, it is well known that much of the labor absenteeism during the war was due to men voluntarily staying away from work in order to seek positions elsewhere that would pay higher wages; and such absenteeism invariably increases the percentage of labor turnover. Mr. Hackett estimates that under normal con-

[1] See J. D. Hackett, "Absenteeism: A Quantitative Study", *Management Engineering*, Feb., 1922, p. 85. Mr. Hackett is Lecturer on Labor and Employment Management at New York University, and President of the Personnel Managers' Club of Queens Chamber of Commerce.

ditions absenteeism will not exceed six per cent and any absenteeism above this is abnormal and preventable. During the war, when there was opportunity for laborers to work overtime and draw time and a half pay for such work, they could often keep up their wage by working a few hours overtime and then absenting themselves from work for one or two days per week. In the investigation where 498,480 hours were worked during the week, 42,480 were overtime hours, and it was estimated that absenteeism accounted for the loss of 89,376 hours during the week.[1] Men who work steadily and are familiar with the machinery are much more productive and, therefore, are less costly to the establishment than substitutes.

Very few establishments have attempted to keep records of the number of absentees, and in cases where such records have been kept, various methods have been used for measuring absenteeism, so that there are few reliable data that can be used for comparative purposes. Some of the establisments that have given special attention to this problem keep in close touch with the employees, and, therefore, keep the pay-roll relatively free from "dead timber", i. e., men who are still carried on the pay-roll, but who have actually severed their connection with the plant; while on the other hand, some establishments make no special effort to eliminate the "dead timber" and count as absentees all whose names appear on the pay-roll, but who do not report for work. Consequently, statistics gathered by these two methods are not strictly comparable and are valuable only as indicating general tendencies.

The amount of absenteeism varies, as in the case of labor mobility, with the climatic conditions, personnel of the plant, character of the business, etc., as well as with changes in industrial conditions. The following table shows the trend

[1] See Hackett *Management Engineering, loc. cit.*, p. 86.

of absenteeism in a representative plant from May, 1916 to April, 1919:

TABLE XVIII

ABSENTEEISM IN AN AUTOMOBILE MANUFACTURING ESTABLISHMENT, MAY, 1916-APRIL, 1919[1]

Year and Month	Average No. of Employees on Pay-roll	Absentees		Labor Flux Per 10,000 Labor Hours
		Number	Percentage[2]	
1916				
May	31294	1962	6.3	4.6
June	32898	1820	5.5	4.3
July	34231	2412	7.1	2.4
August	34012	2443	7.2	1.9
September	35545	1806	5.1	4.7
October	38494	1849	4.8	5.3
November	40439	2055	5.1	1.5
December	40712	1958	4.9	1.0
Average	35954	2038	5.7	6.3
1917				
January	40189	2005	5.0	1.3
February	41189	2344	5.7	1.2
March	40833	2227	5.5	1.2
April	36726	2338	6.4	2.7
May	38373	1677	4.4	3.0
June	36923	1505	4.1	2.5
July	36148	1647	4.6	1.7
August	35886	2571	7.2	2.9
September	35445	1893	5.3	2.5
October	35461	1325	3.7	3.0
November	35124	1087	3.1	2.0
December	34370	1235	3.6	1.4
Average	37223	1821	4.9	2.1

See Emil Frankel, "Labor Absenteeism", *Journal of Political Economy*. June, 1921, pp. 487-499. The table is reproduced on p. 491 from unpublished statistics of the Bureau of Labor Statistics.

[2] Computed by dividing the number of absentees by the average number

TABLE XVIII—*Continued*

1918				
January . .	34040	1621	4.8	1.2
February	33873	1230	3.6	1.2
March	33438	1293	3.9	2.2
April	33318	2117	6.4	4.3
May	33534	1347	4.0	5.8
June	33118	1093	3.2	6.2
July	32701	2402	7.3	3.1
August	32074	1306	4.1	7.2
September	33317	1450	4.4	6.0
October	35503	1905	5.4	7.5
November	37518	2841	7.6	5.5
December	36865	7830	2.1	3.8
Average. . . .	34109	2198	6.4	4 6
1919				
January	36845	2666	7.2	2.3
February	36812	2176	5.9	2.0
March	37967	2629	6.9	5.8
April	41001	2734	6.7	9.1
Average. . . .	38156	2551	6.7	5.0

According to the table, the percent of absenteeism for the period covered ranged from a minimum of 2.1 in December, 1918, to a maximum of 7.6 per cent for the preceding month. There seems to be very little correlation between the labor-flux rates and the percents of abseenteeism, but since the two sets of figures are computed on different bases, they are not comparable except as to general trend.

on the pay-roll. In computing the percentages, it would have been better if the actual number of days that each employee lost had been given, for often the number of days which an employee loses is more significant than the mere fact that he is an absentee. One man might be absent two days while another is absent ten, yet each is reported as an absentee. But in the absence of detailed data relative to the number of days that each worker lost, the method of computation used here gives the best basis for comparison of absenteeism at different times.

It seems that April is, in general, a month of extensive absenteeism, but this is to be expected, since many union contracts end the last of April and workers shift to other employments when not satisfied with the terms of the new agreements which are often drawn up in April. It will be remembered that in discussing the number of strikes, the same influence was found to be present.[1] The large amount of absenteeism in the summer months was probably due to the warm weather.

In a car-building plant employing an average number of 8103 persons, the per cent of absenteeism reached 18.1 in January, 1918, which is explained by the heatless days in cold weather during the month.

Mr. Hackett made a study of the absenteeism of men and women in various industries and found that the percentage of abseenteeism for women was higher than that for men. The results of his study are shown in Table XIX. It would seem from this table that, if absenteeism is responsible for a large per cent of labor mobility, the mobility rate for women should be higher than that for men. This is not the case, however, since much of the absenteeism of women is involuntary, due to illness, bad weather, etc., which are unavoidable on the part of the employee. On the other hand, since men are much more mobile than women, much of their absenteeism is voluntary and results in an increase of labor mobility. Involuntary absenteeism does not usually lead to labor mobility, while voluntary absenteeism does.

[1] See footnote, chapter iii, p. 61.

TABLE XIX

PERCENTAGE OF ABSENTEEISM AMONG MEN AND WOMEN[1]

Nature of Business	Year	Absentees			
		Male		Female	
		Number	Per cent	Number	Per cent
Manufacturing	1919	190	4.52	188	5.75
War materials	1918	9068	10.09	37218	18.40
Shell factory.	1918	. .	5.30	. .	7 80
Unknown	1920	. .	6.01	. .	15 21
Rubber factory.	1919	. .	4.52	. .	8.06
Rubber factory.	1920	. .	4.32	.	7.55

Another investigation of absenteeism in a plant employing an average of 6,700 persons, showed that absenteeism increased during the period of business expansion, and decreased when the depression began.[2] This investigation covered a period of twenty-eight months and included in the beginning, a period of rapid business expansion, and also took in part of the depression. It included the latter part of the first influenza epidemic, and all of the second year of the epidemic. This probably accounts for a large part of the time lost due to sickness. Of the 6,700 persons employed, sixty-five per cent were males and thirty-five per cent females. Classified according to length of service, twenty-eight per cent were employed less than one year, eighteen per cent from one to two years, seventeen per cent from two to three

[1] See Hackett, *Management Engineering, loc. cit.*, p. 87.

[2] R. S. Quinby, "Industrial Absenteeism, Its Causes and Losses", *Management Engineering*, October, 1921, pp. 213-216. See also "A Study in Labor Mobility", *Annals of American Academy of Political and Social Science*, September, 1922, pp. 166-255, and November, 1922, pp. 191-221.

years, twenty per cent from three to five years, five per cent from five to ten years, and twelve per cent over ten years. These figures show that the employees were not unusually restless, but constituted a relatively stable group of workers.

The following table shows the per cent of working time lost by the employees:

TABLE XX

PER CENT WORKING TIME LOST BY EMPLOYEES FROM JANUARY 1, 1919, TO APRIL 30, 1921

Causes	Per Cent of Working Time Lost	Per Cent of All Time Lost
Sickness	2.036	37.06
Industrial accidents	0.139	2.52
Non-Industrial accidents	0.079	1.44
Personal reasons	3.240	58.98
Total	5.494	100.00

According to this table, more time was lost for personal reasons than for any other cause. This is more significant when we consider that the investigation covered two influenza epidemics. It would thus seem that sickness is the cause of the greatest absence from work on the part of the employees. It was found that the men lost an average of five days per year on account of sickness, while women lost an average of eight and three fourths days. The investigation showed that absenteeism due to personal reasons fluctuated with the changes in business conditions, increasing with business expansion and decreasing with the business depression.

While these few isolated investigations are not large or comprehensive enough to be used as proof, they show general tendencies in absenteeism. In general, they show that voluntary absenteeism tends to vary directly with business prosperity and inversely with business depression. The figures show that the laboring class as a whole took advantage of the period of prosperity during the war and increased the amount of their leisure time by voluntarily staying away from work. This tended to increase their dissatisfaction with the old conditions, and caused them to be more emphatic in their demands for more leisure. Their desires in this respect were expressed by their demands for the eight-hour day, and in some instances, for the six-hour day and for a five and one half day week.

CHAPTER V

Changes in Attitude and Policies of Labor, 1915-1922

With the advent of the period of prosperity, wage-earners were not long in taking advantage of their increased strength. Their determination to protect their rights and better their standards and conditions is well illustrated by the following declaration of the Executive Council of the American Federation of Labor, approved by the March 12, 1917, Conference:

Labor has now reached an understanding of its rights, of its powers and resources, of its value and contribution to society, and must make definite constructive proposals.

. . . . Wage-earners in war times must, as has been said, keep one eye on the exploiters at home and the other upon the enemy threatening the national government. Such exploitation made it impossible for a warring nation to mobilize effectively its full strength for outward defense.

We maintain that it is the fundamental step in preparedness for the nation to set its own house in order and to establish a home justice in relations between men. Previous wars, for whatever purpose waged, developed new opportunities for exploiting wage-earners. . . .

We hold that if workers may be asked in time of national peril or emergency to give more exhausting service than the principles of human welfare warrant, that service should be asked only when accompanied by increased guarantees and safe-guards, and when the profits which the employers shall secure from the industry in which they are engaged have been limited to fixed expenses.[1]

The declaration continues with the statement that it is fundamental for the government to cooperate with organized labor for industrial as well as military service, and that labor should be represented on boards and agencies determining policies of national defense. This shows that organized labor, while it had a certain patriotism, was eager to improve its status as much as possible. Labor's demand for reforms increased as time went on, and the feeling of patriotism became less and less influential in keeping down labor demands and labor troubles.

The quotation represents the prevalent attitude of the wage earners during the period of industrial expansion. They saw that this was the opportune time to improve their status and they were determined to do so. They felt that the employers were making large profits, and they, therefore, expected increased remuneration and recognition for their efforts and sacrifices. Mr. James O'Connell, President of the Metal Trades Department of the American Federation of Labor, expressed the idea in a speech before the Boilermakers' Convention in 1917 as follows:

Now I want you to get it into your heads . . . . to talk about dollars, not pennies, in your organization. . . . The opportunity is presented for the first time in the history of the United States Government, practically a union contract signed between the government and the officers of the Department and affiliated organizations, practically requiring that the shipbuilders of America come to Washington and put their feet under the tables with labor leaders to settle their troubles. . . . Uncle Sam is paying the expenses of union committees to

[1] "American Laborer's Position in Peace or in War", *American Federationist*, April, 1917, pp. 269-281.

come to Washington and meet the employers. Isn't that a pretty good union agreement? That is only the beginning.

Now, I hope the Boilermakers, in Convention here, will get in their minds that beautiful thought of "more". Place your officers in a position to go out and demand, and then back them up. Give them your united and undivided support. And in this crisis, instead of our power being lessened, we will come out after the war is over bigger and greater and grander and better understood than we ever were before.[1]

It was soon found that the workers were not satisfied merely with wage increases which, for some industries, tended to lag behind the cost of living. They were demanding representation in industry and redress for long-standing grievances. In other words, they were now fighting for a principle which they were determined to have recognized, namely, workers' representation in those matters in which the wage earners were directly concerned. They began by demanding that labor managers be substituted for foremen. This, it was hoped, would eliminate "driving" and many labor disputes resulting therefrom, by creating a better understanding between employer and employee. Some form of collective bargaining was also demanded that would mean labor representation in fact as well as in name.

During 1917 and 1918, many of the demands of the wage earners were granted by the employers without much opposition. It seemed that both the public, as such, and the employers had taken a more sympathetic and conciliatory attitude toward labor, which promised the dawn of a new era in the history of labor. This was due, first, to the great scarcity of labor during 1917 and 1918. It was a time when interruption of industrial production would be disastrous to the government, for it would interfere with the carrying

[1] From a speech by James O'Connell published in the *Boilermakers' Journal*, Oct., 1917.

on of the war to a successful close; and it would be detrimental to employers from the standpoint of profit. The entrepreneural class as a whole, as well as the government, was eager to avert any labor dispute that might lead to a further labor shortage. It was also realized that at this time strikes were more costly to the employers and the government than to the laborers. When laborers left a plant there were no others to take their places, and there was not a possibility of starving them into returning, because there were too many other places open, and because an interruption in production could not be permitted. In the second place, there actually seemed to be growing up more of a cooperative spirit between the employers and employees. The old type of employer, who believed his business was his to run as he pleased regardless of whom it inconvenienced, had been replaced to a large extent by the new type of employer who realized, at least to some extent, that production is directly tied up with social welfare and should be considered from the standpoint of consumption, as well as of profit. These employers also thought that "driving" by the foreman was a bad policy, since human psychology is such that it naturally resents such methods, and since the organized workers were too strong at this time to be ruled by force. They, therefore, felt that labor efficiency would be increased if the foreman was replaced by the labor manager. This, it was thought, would also help to pave the way for better cooperation between the employer and employee, since the workers now had to be consulted rather than driven.

As soon as the adjustment agencies were created, they took up the problem of settling disputes, and immediately laid down the principle of collective bargaining which was soon quite generally accepted. It took several months to get their machinery for adjustment organized and working efficiently. In the meantime, the employers began to feel that the workers were being granted too many concessions. They also realized that both the numerical and actual strength of the labor organizations was increasing with unprecedented rapidity. Therefore, when the labor shortage was relieved somewhat by women coming into industry in increasing numbers, and especially after the signing of the Armistice, employers made a determined stand against any increase in the powers of labor. Their attitude toward labor soon became almost the reverse of what it was during the first years of the period of prosperity when they were readily granting many of the workers' demands.

The fact that organized labor understood the situation and expected increased opposition from the employers, is shown by the following:

" Before the war was ended, and while, under pressure of war necessity the dominating industrial combinations were compelled to deal with some fairness in their relations with labor, the threat was commonly made, ' wait until the war is over ' ".[1]

Various methods were used, including much propaganda, to combat the growing strength of the workers. The literature of the time was filled with writings on such subjects as " What the Workers Want," " Representation in Industry ", " Reaching the Mainsprings of the Wills of the Workers ", and " Bridging the Gulf Between Labor and Capital ". This unprecedented and widespread interest in the workers' welfare on the part of the employers, during the latter part of the period of prosperity, was due to their desire to forestall a general recognition of the closed shop. The workers contended that effective collective bargaining and the open shop were incompatible, and that harmony in industry between employers and employees was impossible under open-shop

[1] Samuel Gompers, " The Conspiracy Against Labor ", *American Federationist*, Oct., 1922, pp. 721-739.

conditions. The empolyers felt, that by accepting the principles of collective bargaining, they would have the weight of public opinion in their favor, and could thereby better defeat the workers' demand for the closed shop.

As time went on and the workers continued to demand more control and higher pay, at the same time that the soldiers were being discharged and returned to industrial pursuits, their demands were met by greater and more determined opposition on the part of the employers. It was realized that these demands were not mere threats of a few dissatisfied radicals, but that they represented the feeling and desires of a great body of strongly organized workers, headed by extremely able and capable leaders, and backed up by no small degree of favorable public opinion. Especially was this true during 1919 and the first part of 1920, when the struggle reached its height.

Business men were surprised to find that in many cases the workers were better informed on industrial conditions than the employers themselves, and that the labor leaders had scientifically prepared statistics to prove their arguments. They had employed expert economic and legal talent to represent them. Men like Dr. Lauck, of the Bureau of Applied Economics at Washington, were employed to make special studies and present statistics in behalf of the workers.

The employers did not hesitate to take advantage of the increasing supply of labor during the latter part of 1919, and 1920 to wrest from the workers some of the powers and concessions that the latter had gained during the period of prosperity. One method was that used by the United States Steel Corporation in destroying what little headway the workers had made in collective bargaining. The Corporation publicly admitted the right of workers to organize and bargain collectively, but refused to consult with union representatives from the outside. In other words, the United

States Steel Corporation outwardly accepted the principle of collective bargaining, but actually never allowed it to work in practice, because, since outside representatives were barred from meeting with the company officials, it meant that the Corporation dictated the choice of the workers' representatives as well as the votes of these representatives after they were chosen. Many other industries used the same method for breaking up effective collective bargaining, by controlling the election and votes of the labor representatives.

The steel strike was the cause of the calling of President Wilson's first Industrial Conference, and it was the employers' determined stand, headed by Judge Gary, against the rights of workers to organize and bargain collectively through representatives who were freely chosen by both sides, that caused the conference to fail to accomplish any more than it did. They felt that collective bargaining based upon unionism was dangerous to the open-shop principle, which they were determined to protect at all costs.

It was this determination of the employers to enforce open shop conditions, that caused them to adopt collective bargaining in an entirely different form from the way in which it was adopted in England. According to the report of the Whitley Committee, which was the basis of the English system of collective bargaining, both the employers and employees were to organize. The plan called for national industrial councils, district councils, and works committees, all composed of representatives from both sides, and no non-union man could vote or take part in the proceedings. The American plan, on the other hand, was inimical to such councils and rarely extended beyond the individual plants. According to the American plan, the employers refused to deal with trade unions, while in England, the trade unions were the spokesmen of labor, and collective bargaining was, therefore, based directly upon unionism. In other words, the American employers conceived of dealing a fatal blow to trade unions by substituting the shop committee for the union, while in England, the shop committee was merely a supplement to the union.[1]

Never before had the principle of the closed shop and other demands of labor given the employers such grave concern, and never before had they witnessed such an unprecedented increase in union membership. The membership of the American Federation of Labor, as reported at the annual conventions, increased between 1915 and 1922 as follows: in 1915 there were 1,946,347 members; in 1916 there were 2,072,702; in 1917 there were 2,371,431; in 1918 there were 2,736,478; in 1919 there were 3,260,068; in 1920 there were 4,078,740; in 1921 there were 3,906,528; and in 1922 there were 3,195,635. The membership of the Amalgamated Clothing Workers of America between July, 1915 and July, 1921 was as follows: 38,000 in 1915; 48,000 in 1916; 57,000 in 1917; 80,000 in 1918; 138,000 in 1919; 177,000 in 1920; and 143,000 in 1921.[2] This phenomenal increase in union membership between 1915 and 1920 was not to be considered lightly, for the workers seemed to "wax strong" on their own strength, which gave the employers cause for their alarm. The latter were therefore often eager to have disputes adjusted by arbitral bodies, because they felt that the workers would gain less ground by such methods.

One lesson we have learned since the signing of the Armistice, is that compulsory arbitration boards and industrial courts, when questions of principle as well as wages

[1] See Paul H. Douglas, "Shop Committees: Substitute for, or Supplement to, Trade-unions?", *Journal of Political Economy*, February, 1921, pp. 89-107, and A. B. Wolfe, *Works Committees and Joint Industrial Councils*, 1919.

[2] See *Proceedings of the Fifth Biennial Convention of the Amalgamated Clothing Workers of America, 1922,* p. ii of appendix.

and conditions are involved, can not settle wage disputes and bring about industrial peace under normal conditions, unless practiced on a national scale and composed of the most competent men. During the war the various adjustment agencies served a very useful function and prevented many serious labor disputes. But their success was due to a certain feeling of patriotism on the part of the workers, to war psychology, and to generally prosperous business conditions. It was soon seen, therefore, that compulsory or quasi-compulsory arbitration, as used during the war, could not function successfully under peace-time conditions. Certainly " the actions of both the miners and the railroad men have made it abundantly clear that arbitration, by itself, will not serve to keep the peace. For both the railroad shop men and the miners have persistently refused to submit their case to the decision of any arbitral body ".[1] The experience of the Kansas Court of Industrial Relations has given adequate proof that arbitration of this kind can not succeed. But the failure of the Railroad Labor Board and the Kansas Court of Industrial Relations to accomplish what it was hoped they would in bringing about industrial peace, does not mean that arbitration in public service industries is hopeless. According to Professor Seager, there are two main reasons why the continuous operation of public service industries will be facilitated by " the maintenance of an authoritative board or court to determine labor conditions on the railroads and similar state boards or courts to determine conditions on street railways and other local public service industries." [2] In the first place, strikes in industries of this kind are, in the majority of cases, fore-

[1] See A. M. Bing, " The Coal and Rail Strikes ", *American Labor Legislation Review*, September, 1922, pp. 150-154.

[2] See H. R. Seager, " Comany Unions vs. Trade Unions ", *American Economic Review*, March, 1923, p. 3.

doomed to failure, for they usually cause an angered or indignant public opinion to swing to the side of the employers. The latter realize that they can break, aided by public opinion, "any strike that may be started provided the government prevents violence and intimidation on the part of the strikers." [1]

In the second place, the policy of regulating "rates and quality of service" has been accepted, and it is quite a logical step to regulate wages, since they constitute an important item in the cost of production.

The failure of the Kansas Court of Industrial Relations to accomplish the results that its advocates hoped that it would, was probably due largely to the fact that it undertook regulation in too many industries at the beginning, and therefore, increased unnecessarily the probability of adverse criticism. The severe penalties imposed by the law also caused a decided reaction against the whole principle of such regulation.[2]

The Railroad Labor Board, on the other hand, has no compulsory powers and no way of enforcing its decisions except by influencing public opinion by means of publicity. This limitation of the powers of the Board probably kept it from commanding sufficient confidence to give it the commanding personnel upon which its success must to a large extent, depend. Both of these experiments in adjusting labor disputes, have therefore been handicapped by defects in legislation, as well as by conditions which are not yet normal.

[1] Seager, *op. cit.*, p. 4.

[2] In a recent decision of the United States Supreme Court it was held that the Kansas Court of Industrial Relations denies freedom of contract and labor, and, therefore, renders the hopes of compulsory arbitration still less probable. The *New York Times* for June 12 and 13, 1923, comments on the possible effect of this decision. See Charles Wolff Packing Co. *v.* Court of Industrial Relations of the State of Kansas, 43 Sup. Ct. 630, and advance opinions, July 15, 1923, p. 630.

In the past, the employers have followed the theory of *caveat emptor,* and the workers have learned its meaning from sad experience, which accounts largely for their psychology and its resulting manifestations. Theirs is a psychology resulting from balked desires and repressed instincts. This idea has been expressed very well as follows:

> It is in part the abnormal psychology of repression. Broadly speaking, laborers' attitude from time immemorial has of necessity been one of subserviency—a subserviency based on fear—softened and domesticated into a resigned contentment with bread and ball games, but an attitude always charcterized also by thwarted aspirations and repressed pugnacity flaring out at every favorable opportunity in the fierce resentments and reflex violences of slave insurrections, July revolutions, and dock strikes.[1]

There has been too much of a tendency in the past to treat labor merely as one of the factors of production, and the last period of business prosperity tended to emphasize the fact that we can not leave out the human and psychological elements in dealing with workers. They have definite reactions to certain stimuli, and when the period of industrial expansion gave them an opportunity, they showed the result of their repressed instincts by making demands that were considered extreme by many people. Let us see, then, to what extent their demands were unreasonable.

In the first place, their demands for increased wages have been criticised and condemned by many writers as being unreasonable and unjust. This brings up on the one hand, a question of principle, namely, as to whether the return to labor should be limited to a living wage, and on the other, the problem of determining just what constitutes a living

[1] A. B. Wolfe, "Some Psychological Aspects of Industrial Reconstruction", *Publication of the American Sociological Society,* vol. xiv, 1919, p. 68.

wage or proper standard of living. The two questions can not be answered separately, because the answer depends upon the definition of a living wage. The demands of the workers during the war resulted in a definition of a minimum living wage that was acceptable in general to all concerned. The government, the workers, and the employers, the latter represented by the United States Chamber of Commerce, all agreed that a minimum living wage should be sufficient to maintain an average worker's family with a decent standard of living. It would seem that since all were agreed on the definition of a just wage, the question of wages would have been settled; but it was soon found that they could not agree on what wage constituted a decent standard.[1] The question was complicated still more by the rapidly decreasing purchasing power of the dollar. Prices were constantly running ahead of union wages, and thereby causing new disagreements. In the second chapter we saw how union rates tended to lag behind the cost of living. The laborers saw this inevitable tendency, and in an effort to offset the discrepancy between wages and cost of living they demanded an increase in union wages that would make their real wages equal to those in effect before the period of industrial activity. They realized that with the end of the period of prosperity there would be no more bonuses and overtime, and that the union wages would become a maximum instead of a minimum wage. Therefore, they did all that they could to protect their union standards from the inevitable wage reductions that would come with the end of business prosperity, and this was one reason why the workers fought so strenuously to raise their money wage as high as possible.

[1] For a discussion of recent estimates of the living wage, see W. Jett Lauck, "Living Wage Theory Upheld", *New York Times*, Dec. 17, 1922; and Jas. C. Young, "What is the Worker's Living Wage? New Issue of Capital and Labor", *New York Times*, Nov. 19, 1922.

Their efforts to keep their real wages, based on union standards, from falling below their real wages in 1913 meant that they virtually accepted the pre-war union rate as a living wage. The government realized the justice of this demand, and as we have seen, the government agencies, notably the Shipbuilding Labor Adjustment Board, took the wages that were in effect at some pre-war date as a standard to which wage increases were adjusted. The money wages were, in the case of the shipbuilding industry, increased as far as possible to meet the rise in prices after June 1, 1916, so that the shipbuilding worker's real wage would remain the same as it was before our entrance into the war.

The reason why many people thought that the workers were demanding unreasonably high wages, was because they never took into consideration the real wages. It took extremely high money wages to keep real wages from falling. When we consider the wage demands, therefore, in the light of the relation between money wages and the cost of living as shown in the chart on page 34, we must conclude that in general the wage increases were not unreasonably high, but on the other hand, were barely sufficient, if sufficient, for the workers to maintain a proper standard of living. This is true, even though the actual wages tended to increase somewhat faster than the cost of living, since even in those industries where wages increased most rapidly, the increase was often not sufficient to give the workers a decent standard of living, because they were so far below a living wage at the beginning of the period of prosperity.

The Bureau of Labor Statistics has probably made the most careful study of the amount necessary for a proper standard of living, that has been made in this country. The study included the states of Pennsylvania, West

Virginia, Ohio, Indiana, and Illinois. It was "found that the cost of living on the level of health and reasonable comfort varied between $1681 and $1778 a year. When brought down to the price level of September, 1922, the average . . . . was $1728.25 a year".[1] The average hourly wage in 1922 was fifty-four cents per hour,[2] and the union wage was probably lower. In the Cheney Brothers' Silk Manufacturing Company employing an average of 5,428 workers, between 1916 and 1920, the highest rates paid were in 1920 when the workers were receiving an average of 59.4 cents per hour. In a recent nation-wide survey of twenty-three industries, the National Industrial Conference Board found that the average hourly earnings for all employees in September, 1922, was 49.5 cents per hour. If the estimate of the Bureau of Labor Statistics is correct, it seems that wages in general were not unreasonably high according to the requirements of a living standard. For, assuming an eight hour day, a wage rate of between sixty and sixty-five cents an hour was necessary to yield the minimum living wage as estimated by the Bureau of Labor Statistics.

Professor Ogburn estimates that the real wages of common labor declined 9 per cent between June, 1920, and January, 1922.[3] According to the figures of hourly earnings and cost of living as given in Table III, cost of living decreased 3 per cent more than wages between 1920 and 1922. Wages of common labor probably decreased more rapidly than any other because of the large supply of unskilled workers. It should also be remembered that organ-

[1] See W. Jett Lauck, *loc. cit.*, December 17, 1922. These estimates were based upon a family of five as an average sized family.

[2] See Table iv, chapter ii, p. 26.

[3] See W. F. Ogburn, "The Standard-of-Living Factor in Wages", *American Economic Review Supplement*, March, 1923, pp. 118-128.

ization among the workers was very effective in forestalling many wage reductions. Unskilled laborers, therefore, were forced to accept wage reductions more readily than the skilled, organized workers. This was especially true in case of the iron and steel industry.

It was also the discrepancy between wages and cost of living that caused wage-earners in so many instances to endeavor to break their contracts. They felt that they were the irresponsible losers by the change in conditions that they could neither foresee nor prevent. They were severely condemned for breaking their contracts, but they were making a life-and-death fight—a fight for self-preservation—and, even though to break their contracts meant that "agreements became mere scraps of paper", they were forced to bring extreme pressure to bear on unsympathetic employers in order to protect themselves while they had power to enforce their demands. If their real wages failed to keep within a reasonable distance of the cost of living during the period of industrial activity they would lose, and they realized that as soon as the depression began money wages would immediately be lowered and unemployment would increase and they, therefore, would be losers throughout the whole cycle with no chance of making up their losses.

In the light of the circumstances and conditions, therefore, it seems unjust to criticise the wage demands of the workers during the period of prosperity, as being unreasonable. Their wage demands, in general, were both reasonable and just, if measured by the amount necessary to yield a living wage.

Some few have criticised the demands of the workers for shorter hours and better conditions as being excessive. But it is hardly necessary to give much attention to these criticisms by a few people who seemingly are so extremely ignorant of the actual facts and conditions. The efficiency engineers and progressive employers are united in their praise of the eight-hour day. It has been shown that the worker is more efficient and better content and consequently more valuable to the employer, when working eight hours per day than when working ten or twelve hours. Many employers, therefore, adopted the eight-hour day and even the five and a half day week, because they found it paid to do so purely from a business standpoint. The workers have not asked for more than the eight hour day,[1] so it can hardly be said that their demands in this respect were excessive, when the employers themselves found it to be worth while.

In respect to working conditions, no more need be said than that the best of working conditions are never too good, and that as long as any conditions exist that are detrimental to good health and morals, they are dangerous and undesirable from a social point of view and should be remedied. In this respect, the ignorance and carelessness of the workers directly concerned make it impossible for them to better their own status. The public is not aware of undesirable working conditions, and the employers usually will not take steps to better them unless forced to do so by law or by pressure from organized employees, because of the expense involved. Therefore, it is organized labor or the labor movement in general that does much to improve the working conditions of the workers, and brings sufficient pressure and publicity to bear in order to force the employers to remedy unsatisfactory conditions. Instead of the workers being criticised for such work, they should be helped and encouraged, for they are performing a real

[1] The miners demanded a six hour day, but it was in the nature of a demand for the privilege to work six hours rather than a desire to have the day reduced to six hours.

social function by protecting society from many of the evils that necessarily result from poor working conditions.

Another criticism of the workers that was quite general during the period of prosperity, was that they were using their increased power in an effort to gain control of industry. Many people pointed with fear to the closed shop principle as proof of the unreasonable control that the workers were not only demanding, but actually obtaining. But organized labor was neither asking for, nor did it ever expect to obtain, complete control of industry.[1] The workers were merely asking for a form of collective bargaining that would give them a voice in matters of wages, hours, conditions, etc., with which the workers were directly concerned. They never expected to have control of matters of business policy. In other words, organized labor neither expected nor desired that the workers should take over industry, nor that they should dictate to the employer the way in which he should run his business. It was realized by the workers that there were certain business problems and principles that were not of primary concern to the workers and that the employer himself should decide such questions; but they also felt that there were other questions of principle which concerned the workers directly. Such questions they thought, and justly so, should not be decided without consulting the opinion of the workers directly concerned.

The workers were also accused of using underhanded means in an effort to increase their power and control in industry. For example, it was charged that many of the strikes were due to German and radical propaganda, rather

[1] Much of the misunderstanding of the principles and policies of organized labor is due to the fact that the policies of the few radical organizations are often taken as representative of the labor movement in general.

than to low wages and poor conditions. It seems that such ideas were based upon the belief that the workers presented their demands to the government and to the employers, with the understanding that unless these demands were granted strikes would be called and other methods used to hold up production and interfere with the successful prosecution of the war. In speaking of this idea that was causing so much excitement on the part of some people, Judge G. W. Anderson said:

As United States Attorney from November, 1914, to October 15, 1917, I was charged with a large responsibility as to protecting the community from pro-German plots. In October, 1917, I went on the Interstate Commerce Commission; and was until the Armistice in intimate personal association with the Attorney General. . . . Now, I assert as my best judgement, grounded on the information that I can get, that more than ninety-nine per cent of the advertised and reported pro-German Plots never existed. I think it is time that publicity be given to this view. . . . I assert the significant fact that many of the same persons and newspapers that for two years were faking pro-German plots are now promoting 'The Red Terror'.[1]

This criticism of the organized workers and their methods was started by those who were opposed to the labor movement and thought this was a good way to discredit the efforts of the workers to increase their power. But instead of discrediting and discouraging the workers, it merely increased their antagonism toward, and lack of confidence in, the employers and the government. Those who were well informed and open-minded neither felt that the workers were demanding, nor feared that they would obtain, an unreasonable degree of industrial control. Here again, it seems that much of the adverse criticism of labor during

[1] *New Republic*, Jan. 28, 1920, p. 251.

the war was based upon misinformation and was unjust, and probably was one of the contributing influences that tended to cause the workers to lose confidence in the various arbitral bodies and even in the courts, which in turn tended to widen the breach between employers and employees.

It can hardly be said, therefore, that the demands of organized labor in general, as represented by the American Federation of Labor, were unreasonable or against the best interests of the public. In fact, the American Federation of Labor leadership has been called by many, quite conservative, and even those with ultra-conservative views do not class it as a radical organization. The trouble is, that the policies and actions of various radical groups and organizations have been taken as representative of the labor movement, when in fact organized labor as we have defined it, is as much opposed to these radical ideas as are the enemies of the labor movement.

Since the signing of the Armistice, the workers have been dissatisfied with practically every "important wage award", as well as with most of the court decisions in which labor principles and conditions were involved. They have felt, and with much justification, that the arbitral bodies have favored capital. One of the clearest illustrations of this feeling of resentment was shown in the recent strike of the railroad shop men, and the extreme dissatisfaction among the maintenance-of-way men with their wages, although the latter did not strike.

The maintenance-of-way employees did not ask the Railroad Labor Board to raise their wages in proportion to the cost of living as estimated by the Bureau of Labor Statistics, but they did ask the Board to accept the "principle" of adjustment according to changes in cost of living, and also asked the board to make a thorough study of its own in order to determine what constituted a living wage. "Pending the completion of this study, the employees requested a wage rate of 48 cents an hour", which was far below the living rate of between sixty-five and seventy-two cents an hour, as estimated by the Bureau of Labor Statistics.

The board, however, seized upon the rate of 72 cents an hour and used it in an unfair manner to distort the reasonable requests of the railroad workers and to misrepresent and misconstrue their attitude. The board stated that in order to maintain the existing differentials a total wage increase of more than three billion dollars would be necessary if 72 cents an hour was the minimum wage, and that even granting the rate of 48 cents would cost an additional one and one-quarter billion. The figures of the board should be cut in half, and would then still be in excess of the truth.[1]

The intent of the Transportation Act of 1920 was that the railroads should pay a living wage; and the laborers expected the Railroad Labor Board to carry out the letter of the law as it was intended when passed. Such failure of the arbitral bodies to protect the workers, as Dr. Lauck indicates, can not help but cause them to oppose arbitration as a means of adjusting disputes. It causes them to feel that they must rely upon themselves for protection since the government will not help them.

Recent court decisions and injunctions, as already stated, have also had a very decided influence upon the general character of the labor movement. The workers feel that the courts have taken a decided stand against them, and in favor of employers. If the number of decisions and injunctions adverse to the workers' interests, as compared to those against the employers, is an indication of court opposition to the labor movement, it seems that the workers have very good grounds for their belief in the hostility of the courts.

[1] W. Jett Lauck, *loc. cit.*, Dec. 17, 1922.

The disputes between the Amalgamated Clothing Workers of America and the clothing manufacturers during the war and the period of depression following the war are illustrative of the feeling that existed between the employers and employees in general. In 1918 the employers in New York instituted a lockout against the Amalgamated Clothing Workers because of the latters' demand for a forty-four hour week. But the "employers failed to receive the support of some of the large papers, because the latter did not approve of a lockout." In the following disputes the "employers did not wish to repeat the mistakes of 1918 when their own admission of having locked us out brought us moral support from unexpected quarters." [1]

During the period of prosperity the clothing workers began a determined fight for the forty-four hour week and an increase in wages. They felt that the enemies of the labor movement were gleefully rubbing their "hands in anticipation of the after-war unemployment bringing back the old labor conditions, and worse." [2] They also felt that it was incumbent upon them to take steps, while labor was in a strong bargaining position, to meet the inevitable post-war situation. They thought that the best way to meet the situation after the war—when demand for labor would be less and when the supply would be increased by demobilization—was to reduce the number of working hours.

On August 9, 1918, the union formally requested the forty-four hour week but the request was immediately rejected by the clothing manufacturers. On November 9, 1918, the employers declared a lockout against all cutters, and the

[1] See *Proceedings of the Amalgamated Clothing Workers of America, 1920-22*, p. 11

[2] See the *Report of the General Executive Board to the Fourth Biennial Convention of the Amalgamated Clothing Workers of America, 1920*, p. 5.

union immediately declared a general strike. It seemed to be an opportune time for the employers to win and thereby weaken the power of the Amalgamated Clothing Workers of America. But the returned soldiers and sailors immediately joined the ranks of the strikers and, by making public speeches while still in uniform, helped to turn public opinion in favor of the strikers. The employers tried to get the government to prohibit the discharged soldiers from participating in the strike. The effect brought about by the soldiers was a phase of the situation that the clothing manufacturers had not taken into consideration. There was one other point that they had also overlooked, namely, the period of prosperity in the latter part of 1919 and the first part of 1920. Practically everyone expected a depression to follow the signing of the Armistice and the post-war period of prosperity, therefore, could not be foreseen. The manufacturers, instead of preparing for a period of prosperity, were contracting their businesses in preparation for depression. Of course this unexpected rise in prices and increase in business profits after the Armistice was a great help to the wage-earners, especially to the Amalgamated Clothing Workers who were in the midst of a significant labor struggle.

The clothing manufacturers did not wish to lose large profits because of a labor dispute, and, when they saw that the expected depression was not coming, they began to take steps toward bringing about an adjustment of the difficulties. On January 23, 1919, both sides accepted the report of the Advisory Board and the dispute was ended. The employees won a significant victory.

During the depression of 1921, hostilities again broke out between the employers and employees in the clothing trades, and the employers now attempted to use the courts against the workers. In the attempted use of the courts against the labor movement, the employers did not hesitate to make use of the injunction to a greater extent than it had ever been used before.[1] The attitude of the clothing workers toward the increased use of the injunction was expressed in part as follows:

> With the fight between the Amalgamated Clothing Workers and the clothing manufacturers of New York City still in full swing, it fairly rains injunctions hereabouts. The workers seem to be weathering the storm pretty well, but if the number of things they can not do continues to increase, they will have as many disagreements with the courts as with the employers themselves. As far as the public ever sees, an argument between a worker and a judge is a pretty one-sided business; for all that gets into print is what the judge says to the worker when he gets him down.[2]

The Amalgamated Clothing Workers early in 1921 had taken a prominent place in the fight which the opponents of the labor movement had instituted against labor. In January, 1921, a dissolution suit was brought against the Amalgamated Clothing Workers by J. Freidman and Company.[3] The manufacturers asked for dissolution of the union on the grounds that it was "an unlawful combination and conspiracy, organized and existing solely and only for the purpose of preventing the plaintiff and others from exercising a lawful trade and doing lawful acts, and to commit acts injurious to the public welfare, public morals, and trade and commerce. . . ."[4] The dismissal of the suit

[1] Twenty-four injunctions were issued against the Amalgamated Clothing Workers during 1921 and 1922.

[2] *The Freeman*, April 13, 1921, p. 99.

[3] Friedman and Company v. Amalgamated Clothing Workers of America, 115 N. Y. Misc. 44.

[4] See *Proceedings of the Fifth Biennial Convention of the Amalgamated Clothing Workers of America*, 1922, p. 71.

meant the failure of the employers' campaign for the dissolution of labor unions. If the court had upheld the employers in this suit it would have established a favorable precedent for the continuation of such dissolution suits on the part of the employers.

The active opposition of the clothing manufacturers to the Amalgamated Clothing Workers did not terminate with the dismissal of this suit. In March, 1921, Justice Van Sicken, of the Supreme Court of Brooklyn, granted an injunction against picketing by the members of the union.[1] In his opinion, he stated that the courts should stand squarely "as the representatives of capital, of captains of industry, devoted to the principle of individual initiative, . . ." This was the most sweeping opinion rendered in connection with the clothing trades. Other decisions have prevented union pickets from inducing workers, under individual contracts with their employers, from breaking their contracts, but none of them went so far as to prohibit peaceful picketing.

Another important suit in this connection was that brought by Michaels, Stern and Company against the Amalgamated Clothing Workers of America, in May, 1921. A temporary injunction, which was later made permanent, was secured against the Amalgamated Clothing Workers restraining them from resorting to mass picketing in an effort to force "unionization of the shop". The court held that concerted action on the part of a labor organization and its members to compel recognition of a union or redress of grievances, by means of threats, intimidation, etc. is unlawful, and a labor union is liable for damages when its

[1] Schwartz and Jaffee *v.* Amalgamated Clothing Workers of America, 115 N. Y. Misc. 61.

officers and agents, acting within the scope of their authority, encourage such unlawful means.[1]

In the report of the General Executive Board of the Amalgamated Clothing Workers of America for 1922, it was stated that while the union had entered into collective bargaining agreements with the employers and cooperated in every way with the agencies established to maintain normal conditions, "the enemies of the organization were secretly planning for disruption; secretly, until they were ready to come out into the open. The nation-wide anti-labor propaganda furnished the atmosphere, and the growing unemployment, the opportunity, for an attempt upon the life of the Amalgamated."

This feeling of antagonism on the part of the employees was aggravated in the first place, by the methods that the employers used in fighting unionism, such as the system of "individual contracts" which they tried to institute, suits for dissolution, etc. These "contracts" were based upon the United States Supreme Court decision in the case of Hitchman Coal and Coke Company. The antagonism was due, in the second place, to the injunctions that the courts granted the employees' organizations.

The laborers had very good reasons for feeling that the injunction was being used against them in an unjust manner, since each case served as a precedent for the next decision, and it seemed that each succeeding decision tended to limit the legal activities of the workers to a still greater extent. One New York judge, who took a more liberal view, expressed the danger of too liberal a use of the the injunction as follows:

"In an evenly balanced, bitter, long drawn out labor struggle, an edict of the court, leveled at the strikers, shakes

[1] See the *Proceedings of the Fifth Biennial Convention of the Amalgamated Clothing Workers of America, 1922*, pp. 146-150.

the morale of the working men. This is not the purpose of an injunction, although it is frequently, and perhaps generally, the purpose of the employer who seeks it." [1]

It is interesting to note that during the period of prosperity, when the laborers were in an unusually strong bargaining position, there were comparatively few injunctions issued against the workers. A few of the states issued injunctions restraining the laborers from certain acts, but no federal restraining orders were granted until the latter part of 1919, when Judge Anderson issued an injunction prohibiting the officials of the United Mine Workers from calling a stike and distributing strike funds. "The order went further and instructed the officials to have the men return to work". The request for the injunction was based primarily upon the Lever Food and Fuel Control Act.[2] This law was enacted as a war measure "to prevent . . . . scarcity, monopolization, hoarding, injurious speculation, manipulations, and private controls, affecting such supply, distribution and movement; and to establish and maintain governmental control of such necessaries during the war". The court was, therefore, a year after the signing of the Armistice, using war-time measures against labor. The workers resented this action very much, especially when the courts refused to make use of the Lever Act in prosecuting profiteers.

In a recent case, United States v. L. Cohen Grocery Company,[3] decided February 28, 1921, the Court held that the terms of the Act which applied to profiteering were unconstitutional. Cohen Grocery Company was indicted for charging unreasonable prices for sugar, which amounted to

[1] Walter A. Wood Mowing and Reaping Company v. Toohey *et al*, 114 N. Y. Misc. 185.

[2] See U. S. Stat. at Large, vol. 40, p. 276.

[3] 255 U. S. 81, 41 Sup. Ct. Rep. 298.

profiteering. According to section four of the Lever Act as re-enacted in 1919, unreasonable charges are prohibited as follows:

"That it is hereby made unlawful for any person willfully . . . . to make any unjust or unreasonable rate or charge in handling or dealing in or with any necessaries; to conspire, combine, agree, or arrange with another person . . . . (e) to exact excessive prices for any necessaries. . . ."

The Court held that the wording of the section is not clear enough to give information as to the nature and cause of the accusation; and that it amounted to delegating legislative powers to the courts and juries, which violated the fifth and sixth amendments to the Constitution.

When the Lever Act was being debated by Congress, it was definitely understood that the bill should not prohibit strikes and peaceful picketing. In other words, it was not intended that the law should be used against the workers in a way to prohibit their ordinary use of the strike as a weapon of defense. But in fact, the Act was never used against any other class. The workers believed, therefore, that any law the Congress of the United States may pass for their protection will be interpreted by the courts in such a way as to be a detriment to their interests rather than a protection.

Attorney General Palmer issued a public statement defending the position of the government in asking for the injunction.[1] He outlined the trouble that the strike would cause if carried to its logical conclusion, mentioning that it would paralyze transportation, cause widespread unemployment in other industries, and cause great suffering from cold and hunger. The Lever Act was still in force, for the war had not been formally ended.

[1] See *Monthly Labor Review*, Dec., 1919, pp. 69-70.

The Armistice did not end the war and the courts in many cases have held that the war emergency statutes are still in force; the same rule must apply to war emergency contracts. The Congress has held to this position so late as October 22, when an act of Congress was approved making even more effective the Food and Fuel Control Act.

The miners held that, since they had not had a wage increase in nearly two years, and since their wages were not commensurate with the cost of living, a new wage agreement should be negotiated. They felt that the mine owners were as much responsible for the strike as they were, because the owners refused to negotiate a new wage agreement, and they considered that the government was unfair in placing all the responsibility on the miners.[1]

In 1921, the mine owners of West Virginia sought an injunction restraining the United Mine Workers from organizing the non-union mines. Judge Anderson "held that an attempt to unionize the West Virginia mines was in effect an effort to monopolize the coal industry, and that, therefore, the purpose of the United Mine Workers was an illegal one and that all efforts to that end must be enjoined."[2] He went further and enjoined "the enforcement of the performance of then existing contracts between the operators of union mines and the United Mine Workers in the central competitive field with respect to .... the 'check-off' system". The mine workers appealed to the United States court of appeals which suspended the injunction. About the same time Judge McClintic issued an injunction against

[1] See *Monthly Labor Review*, Dec., 1919, p. 62. See also William L. Chenery, "The Coal Strike", *Survey*, vol. 43, November 22, 1919, pp. 150-155.

[2] See *Report of the Proceedings of the Forty-Second Annual Convention of the American Federation of Labor*, p. 40. See also Borderland Coal Company v. International Organization of United Mine Workers of America *et al*, 275 Federal Reporter 871.

the United Mine Workers that was even more sweeping and drastic than that issued by Judge Anderson. In April, 1922, the circuit court of appeals suspended the more 'vicious restraints and continued all other provisions of the injunction issued by Judge McClintic'.[1]

One of the most sweeping injunctions against the laborers was that issued in September, 1922, by Judge Wilkerson against the striking railroad shop men.[2] The court referred to the action of the strikers as a conspiracy against the decision of the Railroad Labor Board, because the shop men refused to abide by the wage decision of the Board. The laborers held that they had a legal right to strike since by the Transportation Act of 1920 the Railroad Labor Board was not given any compulsory powers, and they were therefore not legally compelled to accept the decision of the Board. The injunction restrained the defendants, first from 'interfering with, hindering, or obstructing,' in any manner, the railway companies, or 'their agents, servants or employes in the operation of their respective obligations' in connection with transportation of goods and passengers in interstate commerce. Second, they were restrained from 'conspiring, combining, confederating, agreeing and arranging with each other or with any other person or persons, organizations or associations to injure or interfere with or hinder' the railway companies or employees of the railway companies in the proper conduct of their lawful business of transporting passengers, property, and mail. Third, the order restrained the workers from 'Loitering or being unnecessarily in the vicinity of the points and places of ingress or egress of the employees of said railway companies,

[1] See the *Report of the Proceedings of the Forty-second Annual Convention of the American Federation of Labor*, p. 43.

[2] See *Monthly Labor Review*, October, 1922, p. 176-178. For a discussion of this case see *Monthly Labor Review*, December, 1922, pp. 1-21.

to and from such premises, in connection with their said employment', and from encouraging in any way other persons from committing any of these acts. Fourth, they were enjoined from inducing or attempting to induce, in any manner, 'any person or persons to abandon the employment' of the railway companies. Fifth, they were restrained from picketing or encouraging picketing in any way.[1] The courts had previously held peaceful picketing by labor organizations to be legal, and now the workers were restrained from using this and practically every other means that laborers usually resort to in labor disputes. It shows how far the courts may go in the use of the injunction. The workers felt that the court in this case was depriving them of the only weapons with which they could protect themselves.

These illustrations show what drastic and sweeping injunctions have been used against laborers in their disputes with the employers since the signing of the Armistice. The workers in general, feel that the courts would never have resorted to the use of the injunction to such an extent if it had not been for the laborers' weakened bargaining position due to the depression and consequent widespread unemployment. Their feeling in this respect is strengthened by the fact that the laborers were successful in very few of their attempts to get injunctions against employers.

One of the most successful attempts on the part of the workers to use the injunction against employers was a recent case in New York,[2] in which the International Ladies' Garment Workers' Union and the Joint Board of Cloak Makers' Union of New York City secured an injunction against the Cloak, Suit and Shirt Manufacturers' Protective

[1] *Ibid.*, p. 177. For a discussion of particular phases of this strike see *Railway Age*, July 22, 1922, p. 41; August 12, pp. 275-276; August 19, pp. 341-347; and September 23, pp. 567-570.

[2] Schlesinger *v.* Quinto, Sup. Ct. of New York, 192 N. Y. Sup. Ct. 564.

Association, which prevented the latter from breaking a collective agreement into which they had entered in 1919. The agreement was to be effective until June 1, 1922. Despite the fact that the agreement provided for time-work with a 44-hour week, the employers instituted piecework and a 48-hour week. The court issued an order restraining the manufacturers' association from breaking its contract with the union.[1]

The unions made a few other attempts to secure injunctions against employers, but they were generally unsuccessful. In a few cases they secured temporary injunctions, but the courts refused to make them permanent.[2]

The labor movement has been influenced to an equal, if not greater, extent by the recent court decisions that have been unfavorable to organized workers. In a majority of the cases decided by the Supreme Court of the United States, in which labor principles were involved, the decisions have been unfavorable to labor. There are three very important cases that were decided by the United States Supreme Court between 1908 and 1917 that "thwarted efforts of labor unions to increase their numbers." [3] The first of these, Adair *v.* United States, (208 U. S. 161) annulled an act of Congress forbidding railways or interstate carriers from discharging workers because of union affiliation. The next case, Coppage *v.* Kansas [4] involved the question of the legality of a state law which prohibited employers from re-

[1] See *Monthly Labor Review*, April, 1922, pp. 210-211 and Watkin's *op. cit*, p 327.

[2] See *Report of the Proceedings of the Forty-Second Annual Convention of the American Federation of Labor*, p. 47, and *Monthly Labor Review*, April, 1922, p. 208.

[3] See Thomas R. Powell, "Collective Bargaining Before the Supreme Court", *Political Science Quarterly*, 1918, pp. 396-429.

[4] 236 U. S. 1 (1915), 59 L. ed 441, 35 Sup. Ct. Rep. 240.

quiring agreements from their employees not to become or remain members of labor unions. The state law was declared invalid. This decision was resented very much by the laborers, since a law prohibiting the employers from forcing the laborers to sign undesirable agreements would have been a great protection to the individual worker as well as to the unions. The third case, Hitchman Coal and Coke Company *v.* Mitchell et al.[1] dealt with a situation similar to the case mentioned above. Union officials had been enjoined from persuading the employees to join the union. The operators had coerced the employees into signing individual agreements not to join the union, by making employment conditional on the signing of such an agreement. The court held that the union officials had no legal right to interfere with these contracts, by inducing and encouraging the employees secretely to join the union. There were dissenting opinions in each of these cases and all were opposed to the decisions of the lower court. But the unions were destined to receive reverses at the hands of the Supreme Court that were even more detrimental to their progress than were these decisions.

In 1921, in the case of Duplex Printing Press Company *v.* E. T. Deering et al.[2] the laborers lost much of the protection that they thought had been given to them by the Clayton Act of 1914. Labor had hailed this Act as a great victory for the workers, but the Supreme Court held that it did not legalize the secondary boyoott. The Duplex Printing Press Company refused to recognize the union and refused to pay union wages. Other printing press companies that did pay union wages were then unable to compete with the Duplex Company; and they informed the work-

[1] 245 U. S. 229 (1917), 38 Sup. Ct. Rep. 423, 62 L. ed. 229.

[2] 41 Sup. Ct. 172.

ers that the wages of the other printing-press companies would have to be lowered to meet those of the Duplex Company unless the latter accepted union standards. The employees of the Duplex Company then struck in an effort to force the company to recognize union standards. The strike was ineffective, and the workers then proceeded to boycott the products of the Duplex Company. They encouraged workers to refuse to use the Duplex machines, and the truck drivers refused to haul the machines. The question of the legality of the secondary boycott was before the Court for decision, and the Court held that it was not the intention of those who framed the act to legalize the secondary boycott.

Mr. Justice Brandeis wrote a dissenting opinion in which he held that the workers were justified in their action because they were acting in self-defense rather than with malicious intent. He felt that the contest involved the interest of all whose cooperation was asked; and all those who have a common interest may " join in refusing to expend their labor upon articles whose very production constitutes an attack upon their standard of living and the institution which they are convinced supports it ". The purpose of the Clayton Act, he contended, was to " equalize before the law the position of workman and employer as industrial combatants, and can not be considered unlawful unless done with malicious intent ".

In December, 1921, the Supreme Court rendered another decision that was unfavorable to labor, and that also involved some of the provisions of the Clayton Act. In this case, Traux *v.* Corrigan,[1] plaintiffs operated a restaurant in Bisbee, Arizona, and defendants were cooks and waiters formerly in the employ of plaintiffs. A dispute arose con-

[1] 42 Sup. Ct. 124, 20 Ariz. 7, 176 Pac. 570.

cerning terms and conditions of employment. The union ordered defendants to strike, when plaintiffs refused to yield to the union terms. The defendants picketed and boycotted plaintiff's restaurant. The plaintiffs asked for an injunction restraining the defendants from picketing the plaintiff's restaurant and thereby injuring their business. A judgment sustaining a demurrer and dismissing the complaints was affirmed by the Supreme Court of Arizona. The United States Supreme Court held that concert of action is a conspiracy if its object is unlawful, or if the means used are unlawful; and the means used by the defendants in this case were illegal according to the majority opinion. The Anti-Injunction Law of Arizona, which had been upheld by the state courts was, therefore, held unconstitutional. Three of the judges, Brandeis, Pitney, and Holmes wrote dissenting opinions.[1] Mr. Justice Holmes said: "If, as many intelligent people believe, there is more danger that the injunction will be abused in labor cases than elsewhere I can feel no doubt of the power of the legislature to deny it in such cases." It is because the use of the injunction has been abused, that organized labor is so much opposed to its being applied in disputes between employers and employees. This decision was a great blow to organized labor, and caused the workers to realize more than ever the seeming impossibility of strengthening their industrial position by depending upon the sympathy of the law-making bodies and the courts. But they were destined to suffer what they considered a still greater reverse at the hands of the Supreme Court.

In a recent case, United Mine Workers of America et al. *v.* Coronado Coal Company et al.,[2] decided June 5, 1922, the local union was held liable for the acts of its members.

[1] See *Advance Sheets*, January 15, 1922.

[2] See 42 Sup. Ct. 570, Advance Sheets, July 15, 1922.

The Coronado Coal Company was one of five coal companies that agreed to operate on a non-union basis. This led to a strike of the employees of the Coronado Company, and in an effort to keep out non-union workers, they destroyed some of the Company's property. The Company asked treble damages for this and for an attorney's fee. The Court held that the union could be sued under the seventh and eighth sections of the Anti-Trust Law.[1] Section eight says that "corporations and associations existing under or authorized by the laws of either the United States, the laws of any of the territories, the laws of any state, or the laws of any foreign country", may be sued. According to the majority opinion: "This language is very broad, and the words given their natural signification certainly include labor unions like these. . . . As a matter of substantive law, all the members of the union engaged in a combination doing unlawful injury are liable to suit and recovery". Chief Justice Taft cites with approval the Taff-Vale decision in England[2] in which it was held that the unions were liable for the acts of the individual members; but he fails to state that the decision was ultimately reversed, and that the Trades Disputes Act was passed by Parliament, which makes is impossible to hold the unions liable for the acts of their members.

In the Danbury Hatters' Case,[3] the Hatters' Association had, by boycotting the products of Loewe Company, interfered with interstate commerce, because these products were distributed throughout the various states. The Court held that the union was liable for three times the amount of damages incurred. Section six of the Clayton Act was de-

[1] See Comp. St. Sec. 8829, 8830.

[2] Taff-Vale Company v. Amalgamated Society of Railway Servants (1901), A. C. 426.

[3] See Loewe v. Lawlor, 208 U. S. 274, 28 Sup. Ct. 301.

signed to meet the situation that arose because of this decision. It seems, therefore, that Congress passed a measure to rectify the wrong done by the Supreme Court in the Danbury Hatters' Case, and then in the Coronado Coal Case, the Court swept aside this Act. Mr. Taft went so far as to say:

In this state of federal legislation, we think that such organizations are suable in the federal courts for their acts, and that funds accumulated to be expended in conducting strikes are subject to execution in suits for torts committed by such unions in strikes. The fact that the Supreme Court of Arkansas has since taken a different view in Baskins vs. The United Mine Workers of America, supra, cannot under the Conformity Act operate as a limitation on the federal procedure in this regard.

The decision of the Court not only went further in opposing labor than any previous decision, but stated that the Court was sorry that it was unable to hold the United Mine Workers liable, as well as the local union. This shows the attitude of the Court toward the labor movement, and certainly leaves little hope for the laborers to gain anything from the decisions of the United States Supreme Court until the personnel of the Court is changed, or until pressure of public opinion causes the Court to take a more liberal view. The attitude of the organized workers toward these recent decisions is expressed in part by the Executive Council of the American Federation of Labor as follows:

"The Supreme Court cannot crush this movement without endangering the foundations of society. The workers will not accept slavery, therefore, they will not accept that which makes slavery either likely or possible. They will find a way to preserve those liberties which they have and to gain more as time passes." [1]

Mr. Gompers, in an address before the 1922 Annual Convention of the American Federation of Labor, expressed the attitude of the labor movement toward the courts and the employers, in part, as follows:

We do not becloud our minds, nor do we fool ourselves into any fancied security as to the obstacles which have been and are being thrown across our pathway of progress. On the contrary, we understand the designers and those who carry the designs into effect to weaken the spirit or to crush the hopes of American labor for absolute freedom—we understand them and their purpose just as keenly as they do, and we are just as ready, and perhaps much more so, than are the antagonists of the rightful cause and course of the American labor movement. . . .

Our adversaries term their antagonistic movement the "open-shop," or, cloak it hypocritically, the "American Plan," robbing patriotism of its most glorious name to commit a devilish act. There can be no genuine conference between employers and employes unless the employes stand upon an equal footing of responsibility and power, fearless of the lash of unemployment or discharge because of their consistent attitude toward the people they represent.[2]

It is little wonder, therefore, that the drastic use of the injunction in prohibiting wage-earners from using the strike in their disputes with employers, as well as the adverse court decisions, has caused the organized workers to oppose vigorously any plans for government arbitration of labor disputes. They feel convinced that they must fight any

[1] See *Executive Council Supplemental Report No. 2*, to the 1922 *Annual Convention of the American Federation of Labor.*

[2] See *Report of the Proceedings of the Forty-Second Annual Convention of the American Federation of Labor*, pp. 4-5.

measures that tend to interfere with their use of the strike. The United States Supreme Court has forced them to the realization that they can not expect much from the courts, and the employers have not hesitated in taking advantage of the workers during the depression by lowering wages and fighting unionism. The laborers understand the situation and realize that they must depend upon the strike, which is their best friend and weapon of defense, more than ever. The historical development of the trade union increases their fear, for it recalls "a time when all organizations for the purpose of affecting the labor contract were conspiracies in violation of common law, and they are living in the very presence of court decisions of recent date that threaten the effectiveness, if not the very existence, of unions."[1] The workers realize that they now hold their positions "by grace of the employer" and without any legal protection. Therefore, their industrial status would be endangered if they should accept compulsory arbitration and give up the right to strike, which is the only effective weapon they have. As long as wage-earners continued to work and supply the public with the products of industry, the government will not concern itself with the question of justice; and the workers, therefore, feel that they can not afford to accept a system of compulsory arbitration until they are given some more effective guarantee of protection..

It is not surprising that organized labor has lost confidence in our government and judicial bodies. Time after time they have taken their cases to law, hoping that they would be given legal protection; and time after time, they have exhausted funds that had been collected for strike and benefit purposes, and the courts have decided against them.

[1] See John A. Fitch, "Government Coercion and Labor Disputes", *Annals of American Academy of Political and Social Science*, July, 1920, p. 6.

Even when they win in the state courts or are successful in obtaining favorable legislation, there is small chance that such decisions or statutes will run the gauntlet of the higher courts and be upheld by the Supreme Court of the United States. This has been well demonstrated by the recent decisions that have undermined and taken away the protection to labor that they felt was granted by the Clayton Act. The workers have been disillusioned and shown that the Clayton Act did not change materially the existing rights of employers and employees. The organized workers no longer look upon our courts as instruments of equity when labor disputes are involved, but rather as weapons of oppression. "Through its unwarranted uses and flagrant abuses the courts of equity have become the courts of the rich, the protectors of property and of property rights, and have disregarded the human aspirations and personal rights of the workers."[1]

Organized labor, of course, has a much stronger legal status at the present time than it had several years ago. Since the organization of the American Federation of Labor, for example, the workers have gained additional rights and protection. But the Clayton Act was heralded by the labor leaders as one of the most significant victories that the workers had ever gained. They had rosy views as to the effect of the labor provisions of the Act, and they felt that the question of the liability of the unions for the acts of the members was at last settled in favor of the workers. Some lawyers felt that the Act would not change the legal status of the workers very materially, but others shared the views of organized labor, and thought that since it seemingly was the intention of Congress to give the workers greater protection, the courts, in their decisions, would be influenced in

[1] Fitch, *op. cit.*, p. 48.

favor of labor. The decision in the Duplex Printing Press case, however, indicated rather clearly the attitude of the Court, and the Coronado Coal case merely emphasized just how far the Court was willing to go, and how little the Act affected or modified the status of the workers. When we speak, therefore, of the great reverses that the workers have suffered as a result of the recent Supreme Court decisions, it does not mean that they are in a weaker position legally than they were before the passage of the Clayton Act, but that in the light of what they confidently expected from the labor provisions of the Act, they have suffered great disappointment.

The attitude of the Supreme Court has probably not become any more unfavorable to labor than it has always been. In fact, there have been vigorous and able dissenting opinions in practically all of these important labor cases of recent date. But of course the workers find little solace in the knowledge that there were dissenting opinions in cases which were decided adversely to their interests. These decisions of the Supreme Court are apt to strike us as being more unfavorable to labor than previous decisions because public opinion has become more liberal, especially during the war. The attitude of the judges has probably changed very little, except in cases where the personnel of the Court has been changed, but outside opinion has tended to become more liberal, and in contrast it has made the Court decisions appear less liberal. We can hardly expect a very great change in the attitude of the Court without a change in the personnel.

Those who are opposed to the labor movement, feel that as long as the courts maintain such an attitude toward the rights and privileges of labor, the labor movement can be held in check. It is quite true that these court decisions and injunctions have temporarily weakened organized labor, but they have at the same time increased the antagonism of the workers, as well as the determination of the latter to fight for themselves by using their own weapons.[1] It means that the laborers are going to fight more scientifically in the future. They will be more alert to hire able counsel and carry their contests through the courts in spite of the fact that they have suffered many discouragements and reverses. They will probably be more successful in this respect in the future, because we are passing out of the reactionary period that followed the war, and with pressure of public opinion —together with the appointment of new judges to take the places of the older ones—opinions now held by a minority may become the views of the majority. The workers will also be more inclined to wait for opportune times to strike when their concerted efforts will be most effective.

The opposition to the labor movement during this last depression, as expressed by the employers in their open-shop campaign, and by the courts in their decisions adverse to labor, merely intensifies and aggravates the feeling of antagonism and the spirit of pugnacity on the part of the workers toward employers. It should be realized that wage-earners are human, and that they will retaliate with a spirit of revenge when their rights and privileges, which they have struggled long and valiantly to attain, are taken away from them. They feel their losses more keenly because they are convinced that the Supreme Court, as well as the employers, took advantage of them when they were weakened and placed at a disadvantage by the widespread unemployment accompanying the last period of depression.

It seems for the moment as though the opponents of the labor movement had won a significant victory, but the latter will probably be strengthened by this seeming defeat.

[1] For a discussion of the attitude of organized labor toward the law see Mollie Ray Carroll, *Labor and Politics*, (Boston, 1923), chapter vii.

The period considered revealed to the workers many important ideas. It disclosed to them their great power in periods of prosperity; and it made them realize that their opponents are hard and uncompromising in times of depression. In other words, the first half of the period made it possible for the workers to experience the sensation that accompanies a feeling of power and strength; while the last half forced them to undergo the sting of defeat in seeing many of their hard-earned gains taken away. It is to be hoped that public opinion will soon overcome precedent and cause the courts and employers to take a more liberal-minded and sympathetic attitude toward the labor movement. Progress in this direction may be slow, but since the present opposition is due largely to a reaction after the disturbing conditions of the war, a counter reaction toward liberalism may be confidently expected, especially if business conditions continue to improve.

SELECTED BIBLIOGRAPHY

Books

American Labor Year Book, 1919-1920, and 1921-1922, published by the Rand School of Social Science, New York City.

Berridge, W. A., *Cycles of Unemployment in the United States 1903-1922*. Houghton Mifflin Co., Boston, 1923.

Bing, A. M., *War-Time Strikes and Their Adjustment*. E. P. Dutton and Company, New York, 1921.

Brissenden, Paul F. and Frankel, Emil, *Labor Turnover in Industry*, Macmillan, New York, 1922.

Carroll, Mollie Ray, *Labor and Politics*. Houghton Mifflin Company, Boston, 1923.

Cestre, Charles, *Production Industrielle et Justice Sociale en Amérique*. Paris, 1921.

Commons, John R., *Trade Unionism and Labor Problems*, Second Series. Ginn and Company, New York, 1921.

Gleason, Arthur, *What the Workers Want*. Harcourt, Brace and Company, New York, 1920.

Groat, G. G., *An Introduction to the Study of Organized Labor in America*. Macmillan, New York, 1916.

Hoxie, Robert F., *Trade Unionism in the United States*. Appleton, New York, 1917.

Johnson, F. E., *The New Spirit in Industry*. Association Press, New York, 1920.

Mitchell, Wesley C., *Business Cycles*. University of California Press, Berkeley, 1913.

National Bureau of Economic Research, *Income in the United States*, volume i and ii, Harcourt, Brace and Company, New York, 1921-22; and *Business Cycles and Unemployment*, McGraw-Hill Book Co., New York, 1923.

Slichter, S. H., *The Turnover of Factory Labor*. Appleton, New York, 1919.

Watkins, G. S., *An Introduction to the Study of Labor Problems*. Thomas Y. Crowell Company, New York, 1922.

Periodicals

American Federationist, published monthly by the American Federation of Labor.

American Economic Review, quarterly publication of the American Economic Association.

American Labor Legislation Review, published by the American Association for Labor Legislation.

Annals of the American Academy of Political and Social Science, publication office, Concord, N. H.

Bradstreet's, a Journal of Trade, Finance, and Public Economy. New York.

Commercial and Financial Chronicle, New York.

Harvard Business Review, published quarterly for the Harvard Graduate School of Business Administration by A. W. Shaw Company, Chicago.

Journal of the American Statistical Association, quarterly publication of the American Statistical Association.

Journal of Political Economy, published monthly by Chicago University.

Management Engineering. New York.

Monthly Labor Review, published monthly by the Bureau of Labor Statistics, Washington, D. C.

New Republic. New York.

Political Science Quarterly, edited in New York by the Faculty of Political Science of Columbia University.

Quarterly Journal of Economics, Harvard University Press.

Review of Economic Statistics, Harvard University.

Survey, New York.

Reports

Annual Reports of the United States Labor Department.

Babson's Statistical Tables and Charts.

Decisions of the National War Labor Board.

Interstate Commerce Commission Reports.

Recent bulletins of the Bureau of Labor Statistics.

Report of the Board of Review of Construction to the Assistant Secretary of War, August 31, 1919.

Report of the Forty-Second Annual Convention of the American Federation of Labor.

Report of the Joint Commission of Agricultural Inquiry, October, 1921.

Reports of the National Industrial Conference Board.

Report of the President's Conference on Unemployment.

United States Industrial Employment Survey Bulletins.

Works Commitees and Joint Industrial Councils, 1919, a government report by A. B. Wolfe.

INDEX

Bei Fragen zur Produktsicherheit wenden Sie sich bitte an:
If you have any questions regarding product safety,
please contact:

Walter de Gruyter GmbH
Genthiner Straße 13
10785 Berlin
productsafety@degruyterbrill.com